ASSER'S
LIFE OF KING ⟨

TRANSLATED FROM THE TEXT OF
STEVENSON'S EDITION

BY

ALBERT S. COOK

PROFESSOR OF THE ENGLISH LANGUAGE AND LITERATURE IN
YALE UNIVERSITY

GINN & COMPANY

BOSTON • NEW YORK • CHICAGO • LONDON

The Athenæum Press

GINN & COMPANY • PRO-
PRIETORS • BOSTON • U.S.A.

TO THE FRIENDS

OF

HONEST AND CAPABLE GOVERNMENT

IN AMERICA

PREFACE

The issue of Stevenson's long and eagerly expected edition of Asser's *Life of King Alfred* has provided an opportunity to supply the ever increasing number of the great king's admirers with a more satisfactory rendering into English of this, perhaps the most precious document, notwithstanding all its faults, for the comprehension of his life and character.

The authenticity of the Life was impugned by Thomas Wright in 1841, by Sir Henry Howorth in 1876-77, and by an unknown writer in 1898, and it had become somewhat the fashion to regard it as a production of a later period, and therefore entitled to but little credence. The doubts as to its authenticity have been satisfactorily dispelled by the two eminent scholars who have most recently discussed the difficulties, Plummer and Stevenson.

The former, in his *Life and Times of Alfred the Great,* Oxford, 1902, says (p. 52): 'The work which bears Asser's name cannot be later than 974, and the attempt to treat it as a forgery of the eleventh or twelfth century must be regarded as having broken down. I may add that I started with a strong prejudice against the authenticity of Asser, so that my conclusions have at any rate been impartially arrived at.' The latter, in his noble edition (Oxford, 1904), remarks (p. vii): 'In discussing the work I have attempted to approach it without any bias for or against it, and throughout my endeavor has been to subject every portion of it to as searching an examination as

my knowledge and critical powers would permit. The net
result has been to convince me that, although there may be
no very definite proof that the work was written by Bishop
Asser in the lifetime of King Alfred, there is no anach-
ronism or other proof that it is a spurious compilation
of later date. The serious charges brought against its
authenticity break down altogether under examination,
while there remain several features that point with vary-
ing strength to the conclusion that it is, despite its difficulties and corruptions, really a work of the time it purports
to be. This result is confirmed by the important corrobo-
ration of some of its statements by contemporary Frankish
chroniclers. Thus the profession of belief in its authenticity by such eminent historians as Kemble, Pauli, Stubbs,
and Freeman agrees with my own conclusion.'

   Notwithstanding their general rehabilitation of the work,
however, neither critic is prepared to trust it implicitly.
Plummer says (p. 52): 'On the whole, then, Asser is an
authority to be used with criticism and caution; partly
because we have always to be alive to the possibility of
interpolation, partly because the writer's Celtic imagination
is apt to run away with him.' And thus Stevenson (p. cxxx):
'The work still presents some difficulties. Carelessness of
transcription may possibly explain those that are merely
verbal, but there still remain certain passages that lay the
author open to the charge of exaggeration, such as his mention of gold-covered and silver-covered buildings, if that be
the literal meaning of the passage, and his statement that
Alfred might, if he had chosen, have been king before his
elder brother Æthelred, with whom, it is clear, he was on
most intimate terms.'

   The style of the book is not uniform. The passages
translated from the *Chronicle* are simpler, while in the
more original parts the author displays an unfortunate
tendency to a turgid and at times bombastic manner of

writing. Indeed, it displays, in many passages, the traits of
that Hesperic Latinity which, invented or made fashion-
able in the sixth century, probably by a British monk in
the southwestern part of England, was more or less current
in England from the time of Aldhelm until the Norman
Conquest. This Hesperic, or Celtic, Latinity has been compared to the mock euphuism of Sir Piercie Shafton in
Scott's *Monastery* (Professor H. A. Strong, in *American
Journal of Philology* 26. 205), and may be illustrated by
Professor Strong's translation into English of certain sen-
tences from the *Hisperica Famina,* the production, as it is
believed, of the monk referred to above: 'This precious
shower of words glitters, by no awkward barriers confining
the diction, and husbands its strength by an exquisite balance and by equable device, trilling sweet descant of
Ausonian speech through the speaker's throat by this
shower of words passing through Latin throats; just as
countless swarms of bees go here and there in their hollow
hives, and sip the honey-streams in their homes, and set in
order, as they are wont, their combs with their beaks.'

   With the passage just quoted may be compared an extract
from chapter 88 of Asser, the translation of which is given
below (pp. 49, 50): 'Ac deinde cotidie inter nos sermo-
cinando, ad hæc investigando aliis inventis æque placabi-
libus testimoniis, quaternio ille refertus succrevit, nee
immerito, sicut scriptum est, "super modicum fundamen-
tum ædificat justus et paulatim ad majora defluit," velut
apis fertilissima longe lateque gronnios interrogando dis-
currens, multimodos divinæ scripturæ flosculos inhianter
et incessabiliter congregavit, quis præcordii sui cellulas
densatim replevit.' Such Latin as this is difficult to translate into satisfactory English. If one renders it literally,
the result is apt to look rather absurd; and beyond a certain point condensation is impracticable, or else misrepre-
sents the original, faults and merits alike.

Hitherto there have been three translations of Asser into English — that by J. A. Giles in Bohn's *Six Old English Chronicles,* London, 1848; that by Joseph Stevenson in *Church Historians of England,* Vol. 2, London, 1854; and that by Edward Conybeare, *Alfred in the Chroniclers,* London, 1900. As the basis of my work I have taken the translation of Giles, sometimes following it rather closely, and at other times departing from it more or less widely.

The reader familiar with the traditional Asser will miss some matter with which he is familiar, such as the story of Alfred and the cakes, that of the raven-banner of the Danes, etc. These are derived from interpolations made in the manuscript by Archbishop Parker, which modern critical scholarship has at length excised. For all matters regarding the manuscript, the earlier editions, etc., as well as for copious illustrative notes on the text, the reader is referred to Stevenson's edition.

Insertions made in the text by Stevenson, on what he considers sufficient grounds, are indicated by < >. The chapter-divisions and -numbering are Stevenson's; the chapter-headings mine. Where modern forms of proper names exist, I have not hesitated to adopt them, and in general have tended rather to normalize them than scrupulously to follow the sometimes various spellings of the text. The notes have almost always been derived from Stevenson's edition, whether or not explicit acknowledgment has been made, but now and then, as in the case of the long note on chapter 56, are my own.

YALE UNIVERSITY
July 4, 1905

CONTENTS

ASSER'S LIFE OF KING ALFRED

*To my lord Alfred, king of the Anglo-Saxons, the worshipful and
pious ruler of all Christians in the island of Britain, Asser, least
of all the servants of God, wisheth thousandfold prosperity for
both lives, according to the desires of his heart.*

1. Alfred's Birth and Genealogy.[1] — In the year of our
Lord's incarnation 849, Alfred, King of the Anglo-Saxons,
was born at the royal vill of Wantage, in Berkshire (which
receives its name from Berroc Wood, where the box-
tree grows very abundantly). His genealogy is traced in
the following order: King Alfred was the son of King
Æthelwulf; he of Egbert; he of Ealhmund; he of Eafa;
he of Eoppa; he of Ingild. Ingild and Ine, the famous
king of the West Saxons, were two brothers. Ine went to
Rome, and there ending the present life honorably, entered
into the heavenly fatherland to reign with Christ. Ingild
and Ine were the sons of Coenred; he of Ceolwald; he of
Cutha[2]; he of Cuthwine; he of Ceawlin; he of Cynric; he
of Creoda; he of Cerdic; he of Elesa; <he of Esla;> he of
Gewis, from whom the Welsh name all that people Gegwis[3]; <he of Wig; he of Freawine; he of Freothegar;> he

---

[1] Based on the *Chronicle* under 855.
[2] MS. *Cudam*. So always, but see the *Chronicle*.
[3] Bede, *Eccl. Hist.* 3. 7: 'The West Saxons, formerly called
Gewissae.' Plummer comments in his edition, 2. 89: 'It is probably
connected with the "visi" of "Visigoths," meaning "west," and
hence would indicate the western confederation of Saxon tribes;
... "Gewis" is probably an eponymous hero manufactured out of
the tribe-name.' The *gw* of *Gegwis* is a Welsh peculiarity (Stevenson).

1

of Brond; he of Beldeag; he of Woden; he of Frithowald;
he of Frealaf; he of Frithuwulf; he of Finn <; he of> God-
wulf; he of Geata, which Geta the heathen long worshiped
as a god. Sedulius makes mention of him in his metrical
Paschal Poem, as follows:

> If heathen poets rave o'er fancied woe,
> While in a turgid stream their numbers flow —
> Whether the tragic buskin tread the stage,
> Or waggish Geta all our thoughts engage;
> If by the art of song they still revive
> The taint of ill, and bid old vices live;
> If monumental guilt they sing, and lies
> Commit to books in magisterial wise;
> Why may not I, who list to David's lyre,
> And reverent stand amid the hallowed choir,
> Hymn heavenly things in words of tranquil tone,
> And tell the deeds of Christ in accents all my own?

This Geata was the son of Tætwa; he of Beaw; he of
Sceldwea; he of Heremod; he of Itermod; he of Hathra;
he of Hwala; he of Bedwig; he of Sceaf[1]; he of Noah; he
of Lamech; he of Methuselah; he of Enoch; <he of Jared>;
he of Mahalalel; he of Kenan[2]; he of Enosh; he of Seth;
he of Adam.

2. Genealogy of Alfred's Mother.[3] — The mother of Alfred
was named Osburh, an extremely devout woman, noble
in mind, noble also by descent; she was daughter to Oslac,
the famous cupbearer of King Æthelwulf. This Oslac

---

[1] MS., Stev. *Seth* (but Stevenson suggests *Sceaf* in his variants, referring to the *Chronicle* under 855).

[2] MS. *Cainan*, but see Gen. 5. 12 in R. V.

[3] Partly from the *Chronicle*, but the whole account of Alfred's father and mother is original.

was a Goth by nation, descended from the Goths and Jutes — of the seed, namely, of Stuf and Wihtgar, two brothers and ealdormen. They, having received possession of the Isle of Wight from their uncle, King Cerdic, and his son Cynric their cousin,[1] slew the few British inhabitants whom they could find in that island, at a place called Wihtgaraburg[2]; for the other inhabitants of the island had either been slain or had escaped into exile.

3. The Danes at Wicganbeorg and Sheppey.[3] — In the year of our Lord's incarnation 851, which was the third of King Alfred's life, Ceorl, Ealdorman of Devon, fought with the men of Devon against the heathen at a place called Wicganbeorg,[4] and the Christians gained the victory. In that same year the heathen first wintered in the island called Sheppey, which means 'Sheep-island,' situated in the river Thames between Essex and Kent, though nearer to Kent than to Essex, and containing a fair monastery.[5]

4. The Danes sack Canterbury.[6] — The same year a great army of heathen came with three hundred and fifty ships to the mouth of the river Thames, and sacked Dorubernia, or Canterbury,[7] <and also London> (which lies on the north bank of the river Thames, on the confines of Essex and Middlesex, though in truth that city belongs to Essex); and they put to flight Beorhtwulf, King of Mercia, with all the army which he had led out to oppose them.

---

[1] From the *Chronicle* under 530 and 534.

[2] Unidentified.

[3] From the *Chronicle*.

[4] Possibly Wigborough, in the parish of South Petherton in Somersetshire (Stevenson).

[5] Minster in Sheppey, founded by St. Sexburh in the seventh century; it disappeared during the Danish ravages (Stevenson).

[6] From the *Chronicle*.

[7] MS. *Cantwariorum civitatem*; Chron. *Cantwaraburg.*

5. Battle of Aclea.[1] — Having done these things there, the aforesaid heathen host went into Surrey, which is a shire situated on the south shore of the river Thames, and to the west of Kent. And Æthelwulf, King of the Saxons, and his son Æthelbald, with the whole army, fought a long time against them at a place called Aclea,[2] that is, 'Oak-plain'; there, after a lengthy battle, which was fought with much bravery on both sides, the most part of the heathen horde was utterly destroyed and slain, so that we never heard of their being so smitten, either before or since, in any region, in one day[3]; and the Christians gained an honorable victory, and kept possession of the battle-field.

6. Defeat of the Danes at Sandwich.[4] — In that same year Æthelstan and Ealdorman Ealhere slew a large army of the heathen in Kent, at a place called Sandwich, and took nine ships of their fleet, the others escaping by flight.

7. Æthelwulf assists Burgred.[5] — In the year of our Lord's incarnation 853, which was the fifth of King Alfred's life, Burgred, King of the Mercians, sent messengers to beseech Æthelwulf, King of the West Saxons, to come and help him in reducing to his sway the inhabitants of Mid-Wales, who dwell between Mercia and the western sea, and who were struggling against him beyond measure. So without delay King Æthelwulf, on receipt of the embassy, moved his army, and advanced with King Burgred against Wales[6];

---

[1] Based upon the *Chronicle*.

[2] Stevenson is inclined to reject this customary identification with Oakley, in Surrey.

[3] The source — the *Chronicle* — says: 'And there made the greatest slaughter among the heathen army that we have heard reported to the present day.'

[4] From the *Chronicle*.

[5] Mainly from the *Chronicle*.

[6] The 'North Welsh' of the *Chronicle*.

and immediately upon his entrance he ravaged it, and reduced it under subjection to Burgred. This being done, he returned home.

8. Alfred at Rome.[1] — In that same year King Æthelwulf sent his above-named son Alfred to Rome, with an honorable escort both of nobles and commoners. Pope Leo at that time presided over the apostolic see, and he anointed as king[2] the aforesaid child[3] Alfred in the town, and, adopting him as his son, confirmed him.[4]

9. Other Events of 853.[5] — That same year also, Ealdorman Ealhere with the men of Kent, and Huda with the men of Surrey, fought bravely and resolutely against an army of the heathen in the island which is called Tenet[6] in the Saxon tongue, but Ruim in the Welsh language. At first the Christians were victorious. The battle lasted a long time; many fell on both sides, and were drowned in the water; and both the ealdormen were there slain. In the same year also, after Easter, Æthelwulf, King of the West Saxons, gave his daughter to Burgred, King of the Mercians, as his queen, and the marriage was celebrated in princely wise at the royal vill of Chippenham.

---

[1] Based upon the *Chronicle*.

[2] MS. *in regem.*   [3] MS. *infantem.*

[4] 'A letter from the pope to Alfred's father, regarding the ceremony at Rome, has been fortunately preserved for us in a twelfth-century collection of papal letters, now in the British Museum. . . . The letter is as follows: "*Edeluulfo, regi Anglorum* [marginal direction for rubricator]. <F>ilium vestrum Erfred, quem hoc in tempore ad Sanctorum Apostolorum limina destinare curastis, benigne suscepimus, et, quasi spiritalem filium consulatus cingulo <cinguli *emend. Ewald*> honore vestimentisque, ut mos est Romanis consulibus, decoravimus,eo quod in nostris se tradidit manibus"' (Stevenson). The *Chronicle* has: '. . . consecrated him as king, and took him as bishop-son.' See p. 29.

[5] Based upon the *Chronicle*.   [6] Thanet.

10. The Heathen winter in Sheppey.[1] — In the year of our Lord's incarnation 855, which was the seventh of the aforesaid king's life, a great army of the heathen spent the whole winter in the aforesaid island of Sheppey.

11. Æthelwulf journeys to Rome.[2] — In that same year the aforesaid worshipful King Æthelwulf freed the tenth part of all his kingdom from every royal service and tribute, and offered it up as an everlasting grant to God the One and Three, on the cross of Christ, for the redemption of his own soul and those of his predecessors. In the same year he went to Rome with much honor; and taking with him his son, the aforesaid King Alfred, a second time on the same journey, because he loved him more than his other sons, he remained there a whole year. After this he returned to his own country, bringing with him Judith, daughter of Charles, King of the Franks.[3]

12. Rebellion of Æthelbald.[4]—In the meantime, however, whilst King Æthelwulf was residing this short time beyond sea, a base deed was done in the western part of Selwood,[5] repugnant to the morals of all Christians. For King Æthelbald, Ealhstan, Bishop of the church of Sherborne, and Eanwulf, Ealdorman of Somerset, are said to have formed a conspiracy to the end that King Æthelwulf, on his return from Rome, should not again be received in his kingdom. This unfortunate occurrence, unheard-of in all previous ages, is ascribed by many to the bishop and ealdorman alone, since, say they, it resulted from their counsels. Many also ascribe it solely to the insolence of the king, because he was headstrong in this matter and in many other perversities, as I have heard related by certain persons, and as was

---

[1] From the *Chronicle.*   [2] Based upon the *Chronicle.*
[3] Charles the Bald.   [4] Original,
[5] Comprising Somerset, Devon, and Cornwall.

proved by the result of that which followed. For on his return from Rome, Æthelwulf's son aforesaid, with all his counselors, or rather waylayers, attempted to perpetrate the crime of repulsing the king from his own kingdom; but neither did God suffer it, nor did the nobles of all Wessex consent thereto. For to prevent this irremediable danger to Wessex of a war between father and son, or rather of the whole nation waging civil war more fiercely and cruelly from day to day, as they espoused the cause of the one or the other, — by the extraordinary clemency of the father, seconded by the consent of all the nobles, the kingdom which had hitherto been undivided was parted between the two, the eastern districts being given to the father, and the western to the son. Thus where the father ought by just right to have reigned, there did his unjust and obstinate son bear rule; for the western part of Wessex is always superior to the eastern.

13. Judith's Position in Wessex.[1] — When Æthelwulf, therefore, returned from Rome, the whole nation, as was fitting, so rejoiced[2] in the arrival of the ruler that, if he had allowed them, they would have expelled his unruly son Æthelbald, with all his counselors, from the kingdom. But he, as I have said, acting with great clemency and prudent counsel, would not act in this way, lest the kingdom should be exposed to peril. He likewise bade Judith, daughter of King Charles, whom he had received from her father, take her seat by his own side on the royal throne, without any dispute or enmity from his nobles even to the end of his life, though contrary to the perverse custom of that nation.[3]

---

[1] Chiefly original.   [2] From the *Chronicle*.
[3] Prudentius of Troyes (in *Annales Bertiniani*, an. 856, ed. Waitz, p. 47), says of Bishop Hincmar: 'Eam . . . reginæ nomine insignit, quod sibi suæque genti eatenus fuerat insuetum.'

For the nation of the West Saxons does not allow the
queen to sit beside the king, nor to be called queen, but
only the king's wife; which refusal, or rather reproach,
the chief persons of that land say arose from a certain
headstrong and malevolent queen of the nation, who did
all things so contrary to her lord and to the whole people
that not only did the hatred which she brought upon herself bring to pass her exclusion from the queenly throne,
but also entailed the same corruption upon those who came
after her, since, in consequence of the extreme malignity of
that queen, all the inhabitants of the land banded themselves together by an oath never in their lives to let any
king reign over them who should bid his queen take her seat
on the royal throne by his side. And because, as I think,
it is not known to many whence this perverse and detest-
able custom first arose in Wessex, contrary to the custom
of all the Germanic peoples, it seems to me right to explain
it a little more fully, as I have heard it from my lord Alfred
the truth-teller, King of the Anglo-Saxons, who often told
me about it, as he also had heard it from many men
of truth who related the fact, or, I should rather say,
expressly preserved the remembrance of it.

14. Offa and Eadburh.[1] — There was in Mercia in recent
times a certain valiant king, who was dreaded by all the
neighboring kings and states. His name was Offa, and it
was he who had the great dike made from sea to sea
between Wales and Mercia.[2] His daughter, named Eadburh,
was married to Beorhtric, King of the West Saxons. The
moment she had possessed herself of the king's good will,
and practically the whole power of the realm, she began to

---

[1] Original.
[2] Offa's Dike; it extended from the mouth of the Dee to that of the
Severn.

live tyrannically, after the manner of her father. Every
man whom Beorhtric loved she would execrate, and would
do all things hateful to God and man, accusing to the king
all whom she could, thus depriving them insidiously either
of life or of power. And if she could not obtain the king's
consent, she used to take them off by poison, as is ascertained
to have been the case with a certain young man beloved by
the king, whom she poisoned, seeing that she could not
accuse him to the king. It is said, moreover, that King
Beorhtric unwittingly tasted of the poison, though the queen
had intended to give it, not to him, but to the young man;
the king, however, was beforehand with him, and so both
perished.

15. Eadburh's Further Life.[1] — King Beorhtric therefore
being dead, the queen, since she could no longer remain
among the Saxons, sailed beyond sea with countless treasures, and came to Charles,[2] King of the Franks. As she
stood before the dais, bringing many gifts to the king, Charles
said to her: 'Choose, Eadburh, between me and my son, who
stands with me on this dais.' She, without deliberation, fool-
ishly replied: 'If I am to have my choice, I choose your son,
because he is younger than you.' At which Charles smiled
and answered: 'If you had chosen me, you should have had
my son; but since you have chosen him, you shall have
neither me nor him.' However, he gave her a large convent
of nuns, in which, having laid aside her secular habit, and
assumed the dress worn by the nuns, she discharged the
office of abbess for a few years. As she is said to have
lived irrationally in her own country, so she appears to
have acted much more so among a foreign people; for, being
finally caught in illicit intercourse with a man of her own
nation, she was expelled from the monastery by order of

---

[1] Original.   [2] Charlemagne.

King Charles. Henceforward she lived a life of shame in poverty and misery until her death; so that at last, accompanied only by one slave, as I have heard from many who saw her, she begged her bread daily at Pavia,[1] and so wretchedly died.

16. Æthelwulf's Will.[2] — Now King Æthelwulf lived two years after his return from Rome; during which, among many other good deeds of this present life, reflecting on his departure according to the way of all flesh, that his sons might not quarrel unreasonably after their father's death, he ordered a will or letter of instructions to be written,[3] in which he commanded that his kingdom should be duly divided between his two eldest sons; his private heritage between his sons, his daughter, and his relatives; and the money which he should leave behind him between his soul [4] and his sons and nobles. Of this prudent policy I have thought fit to record a few instances out of many for posterity to imitate, namely, such as are understood to belong principally to the needs of the soul; for the others, which relate only to human stewardship, it is not necessary

[1] 'Pavia was on the road to Rome, and was hence frequented by English pilgrims on their journey to the latter' (Stevenson). The *Chronicle* says under 888: 'Queen Æthelswith, who was King Alfred's sister, died; *and her body lies at Pavia.*' 'With this story of Eadburh's begging in that city we may compare the statement of St. Boniface, written about 747, as to the presence of English prostitutes or adulteresses in the cities of Lombardy, Frankland, or Gaul (Dümmler, *Epistolæ Karolini Ævi* 1. 355; Haddan and Stubbs, *Councils* 3. 381). At the date of this letter the Lombards still spoke their native Germanic tongue, and it is probable that as late as Eadburh's time it was still the predominant speech in Lombardy' (Stevenson).

[2] Mostly original.

[3] In Alfred's will (*Cart. Sax.* 2. 177. 9) he refers to this as 'Aþulfes cinges yrfegewrit' (Stevenson).

[4] That is, for the good of his soul.

to insert in this little work, lest prolixity should create disgust in those who read or wish to hear. For the benefit of his soul, then, which he studied to promote in all things from the first flower of his youth, he directed that, through all his hereditary land, one poor man to every ten hides,[1] either native or foreigner, should be supplied with food, drink, and clothing by his successors unto the final Day of Judgment; on condition, however, that that land should still be inhabited both by men and cattle, and should not become deserted. He commanded also a large sum of money, namely, three hundred mancuses,[2] to be carried annually to Rome for the good of his soul, to be there distributed in the following manner: a hundred mancuses in honor of St. Peter, especially to buy oil for the lights of that apostolic church on Easter Eve, and also at cockcrow; a hundred mancuses in honor of St. Paul, for the same purpose of buying oil for the church of St. Paul the apostle, to fill the lamps for Easter Eve and cockcrow; and a hundred mancuses for the universal apostolic Pope.

17. Æthelbald marries Judith.[3] — But when King Æthelwulf was dead <and buried at Winchester),[4] his son Æthelbald, contrary to God's prohibition and the dignity of a Christian, contrary also to the custom of all the heathen,[5] ascended his father's bed, and married Judith, daughter of Charles, King of the Franks, incurring much infamy from all who heard of it. During two years and a half of

---

[1] Lat. *manentibus.*
[2] A mancus was thirty pence, one-eighth of a pound.
[3] Original.
[4] From Florence of Worcester. The *Annals of St. Neots* have: 'and buried at Steyning' (*Stemrugam*).
[5] This last statement is incorrect.

lawlessness he held after his father the government of the West Saxons.

18. Æthelbert's Reign.[1] — In the year of our Lord's incarnation 860, which was the twelfth of King Alfred's life, <King> Æthelbald <died, and) was buried at Sherborne. His brother Æthelbert, as was right, added Kent, Surrey, and Sussex to his realm. In his days a great army of heathen came from the sea, and attacked and laid waste the city of Winchester. As they were returning laden with booty to their ships, Osric, Ealdorman of Hampshire, with his men, and Ealdorman Æthelwulf, with the men of Berkshire, faced them bravely. Battle was then joined in the town, and the heathen were slain on every side; and finding themselves unable to resist, they took to flight like women, and the Christians held the battle-field.

19. Æthelbert's Death.[2] — So Æthelbert governed his kingdom five years in peace and love and honor; and went the way of all flesh, to the great grief of his subjects. He rests interred in honorable wise at Sherborne, by the side of his brother.

20. The Danes in Kent.[3] — In the year of our Lord's incarnation 864 the heathen wintered in the isle of Thanet, and made a firm treaty with the men of Kent, who promised them money for observing their agreement. In the meantime, however, the heathen, after the manner of foxes, burst forth with all secrecy from their camp by night, and setting at naught their engagements, and spurning the promised money — which they knew was less than they

---

[1] From the *Chronicle* under 860. As Æthelbert was already in possession of Kent, Surrey, and Sussex, it should rather be said that he added Wessex.

[2] From the *Chronicle* under 860.

[3] Chiefly from the *Chronicle* under 865 and 866.

could get by plunder — they ravaged all the eastern coast
of Kent.

21. Æthelred's Accession.[1] — In the year of our Lord's incarnation 866, which was the eighteenth of King Alfred's
life, Æthelred, brother of King Æthelbert, undertook the
government of the West Saxon realm. The same year a
great fleet of heathen came to Britain from the Danube,[2]
and wintered in the kingdom of the East Saxons, which
is called in Saxon East Anglia; and there they became in
the main an army of cavalry. But, to speak in nautical
phrase, I will no longer commit my vessel to wave and
sail, or steer my roundabout course at a distance from land
through so many calamities of wars and series of years, but
rather return to that which first prompted me to this task:
that is to say, I think it right briefly to insert in this place
the little that has come to my knowledge about the character of my revered lord Alfred, King of the Anglo-Saxons,
during the years of infancy and boyhood.

22. Alfred's Rearing.[3] — He was extraordinarily beloved
by both his father and mother, and indeed by all the people, beyond all his brothers; in inseparable companionship
with them he was reared at the royal court.[4] As he advanced through the years of infancy and youth, he appeared
more comely in person than his brothers, as in counte-
nance, speech, and manners he was more pleasing than
they. His noble birth and noble nature implanted in him
from his cradle a love of wisdom above all things, even
amid all the occupations of this present life; but — with
shame be it spoken! — by the unworthy neglect of his

---

[1] The earlier part from the *Chronicle*.
[2] Probably meaning the mouths of the Rhine (Stevenson).
[3] Original.
[4] *Curto*, a word showing Frankish influence.

parents and governors he remained illiterate till he was twelve years old or more, though by day and night he was an attentive listener to the Saxon poems which he often heard recited, and, being apt at learning, kept them in his memory. He was a zealous practiser of hunting in all its branches, and followed the chase with great assiduity and success; for his skill and good fortune in this art, and in all the other gifts of God, were beyond those of every one else, as I have often witnessed.

23. Alfred and the Book of Saxon Poems.[1] — Now on a certain day his mother was showing him and his brothers a book of Saxon poetry, which she held in her hand, and finally said: 'Whichever of you can soonest learn this volume, to him will I give it.' Stimulated by these words, or rather by divine inspiration, and allured by the beautifully illuminated letter at the beginning of the volume, <Alfred>[2] spoke before all his brothers, who, though his seniors in age, were not so in grace, and answered his mother: 'Will you really give that book to that one of us who can first understand and repeat it to you ?' At this his mother smiled with satisfaction, and confirmed what she had before said: 'Yes,' said she, 'that I will.' Upon this the boy took the book out of her hand, and went to his master and learned it by heart,[3] whereupon he brought it back to his mother and recited it.

24. Alfred's Handbook.[4]— After this <he learned>[2] the daily course, that is, the celebration of the hours, and afterwards certain Psalms, and many prayers, contained in a book[5] which he kept day and night in his bosom, as

---

[1] Original. Stevenson would refer this event to a date earlier than 855.   [2] From Florence of Worcester.

[3] So Pauli and Stevenson interpret *legit.*

[4] Original.   [5] Cf. chap. 88.

I myself have seen, and always carried about with him,
for the sake of prayer, through all the bustle and business
of this present life. But, sad to relate, he could not gratify
his ardent wish to acquire liberal art,[1] because, as he was
wont to say, there were at that time no good teachers in
all the kingdom of the West Saxons.[2]

25. Alfred's Love of Learning.[3] — This he would confess,
with many lamentations and with sighs from the bottom
of his heart, to have been one of his greatest difficulties
and impediments in this present life, that when he was
young and had leisure and capacity for learning, he had no
masters; but when he was more advanced in years, he was
continually occupied, not to say harassed, day and night,
by so many diseases unknown to all the physicians of this
island, as well as by internal and external anxieties of
sovereignty, and by invasions of the heathen by sea and
land, that though he then had some store of teachers and
writers,[4] it was quite impossible for him to study. But yet
among the impediments of this present life, from childhood to the present day [and, as I believe, even until his
death],[5] he has continued to feel the same insatiable desire.

---

[1] The liberal arts were seven, consisting of the *trivium* — grammar,
logic, and rhetoric — and the *quadrivium* — arithmetic, geometry,
music, and astronomy. This course of study was introduced in the
sixth century. Asser here employs the singular, *artem*, which might
be translated by 'education.'

[2] See Alfred's own statement in Appendix I, p. 69.

[3] Original.

[4] Alfred says (Preface to the *Pastoral Care*): 'Thanks be to
Almighty God that we have any teachers among us now.' In this
same Preface he mentions, among those who aided him in the translation. Archbishop Plegmund, Bishop Asser, our author, and the two
priests Grimbold and John. Cf. chaps. 77, 78, 79, 81, 88, and
Appendix I, p. 71.   [5] Stevenson brackets this clause.

26. The Danes occupy York.[1] — In the year of our Lord's incarnation 867, which was the nineteenth of the aforesaid King Alfred's life, the army of heathen before mentioned removed from East Anglia to the city of York, which is situated on the north bank of the river Humber.

27. Defeat of the Northumbrians.[1] — At that time a violent discord arose, by the instigation of the devil, among the Northumbrians, as always is wont to happen to a people who have incurred the wrath of God. For the Northumbrians at that time, as I have said,[2] had expelled their lawful king Osbert from his realm, and appointed a certain tyrant named Ælla, not of royal birth, over the affairs of the kingdom. But when the heathen approached, by divine providence, and the furtherance of the common weal by the nobles, that discord was a little appeased, and Osbert and Ælla uniting their resources, and assembling an army, marched to the town of York. The heathen fled at their approach, and attempted to defend themselves within the walls of the city. The Christians, perceiving their flight and the terror they were in, determined to follow them within the very ramparts of the town, and to demolish the wall; and this they succeeded in doing, since the city at that time was not surrounded by firm or strong walls. When the Christians had made a breach, as they had purposed, and many of them had entered into the city along with the heathen, the latter, impelled by grief and necessity, made a fierce sally upon them, slew them, routed them, and cut them down, both within and without the walls. In that battle fell almost all the Northumbrian

---

[1] Mostly from the *Chronicle*.

[2] This clause must refer to the first line of the chapter, as there is no previous mention of the Northumbrians.

troops, and both the kings were slain; the remainder, who escaped, made peace with the heathen.

28. Death of Ealhstan.[1] — In the same year, Ealhstan, Bishop of the church of Sherborne, went the way of all flesh, after he had honorably ruled his see fifty years; and in peace he was buried at Sherborne.

29. Alfred marries.[2] — In the year of our Lord's incarnation 868, which was the twentieth of King Alfred's life, the aforesaid revered King Alfred, then occupying only the rank of viceroy (*secundarii*), betrothed[3] and espoused a noble Mercian lady,[4] daughter of Æthelred, surnamed Mucill, Ealdorman of the Gaini.[5] The mother of this lady was named Eadburh, of the royal line of Mercia, whom I often saw with my own eyes a few years before her death. She was a venerable lady, and after the decease of her husband remained many years a chaste widow, even till her own death.

30. The Danes at Nottingham.[6] — In that same year the above-named army of heathen, leaving Northumbria, invaded Mercia, and advanced to Nottingham, which is called in Welsh Tigguocobauc,[7] but in Latin 'The House of Caves,'

---

[1] From the *Chronicle*.   [2] Original.

[3] '*Subarravit*, formed from *sub* and *arrha*, represents literally the English verb *wed*, which refers to the giving of security upon the engagement of marriage. . . . [It] is glossed by *beweddian* in Napier's *Old English Glosses*' (Stevenson).

[4] William of Malmesbury calls her Æthelswith.

[5] Of the Gaini nothing is known.

[6] Largely from the *Chronicle*.

[7] 'A compound of *tig* (Modern Welsh *tŷ*, "house"), and *guocobauc* (Modern Welsh *gogofawg*), an adjective derived from *gogof*, "cave." . . . The name . . . is certainly applicable to Nottingham, which has long been famous for the houses excavated out of the soft sandstone upon which it stands' (Stevenson). The word Nottingham itself, however, has not this meaning.

and wintered there that same year. Immediately on their
approach, Burgred, King of the Mercians, and all the
nobles of that nation, sent messengers to Æthelred,[1] King
of the West Saxons, and his brother Alfred, entreating
them to come and aid them in fighting against the aforesaid army. Their request was readily granted; for the
brothers, as soon as promised, assembled an immense army
from every part of their <realm>, and, entering Mercia, came
to Nottingham, all eager for battle. When now the heathen,
defended by the castle, refused to fight, and the Christians
were unable to destroy the wall, peace was made between
the Mercians and the heathen, and the two brothers,
Æthelred and Alfred, returned home with their troops.

31. The Danes at York.[2] — In the year of our Lord's incarnation 869, which was the twenty-first of King Alfred's life,
the aforesaid army of heathen, riding back to Northumbria,
went to the city of York, and there passed the whole winter.

32. The Danes at Thetford.[2] — In the year of our Lord's
incarnation 870, which was the twenty-second of King
Alfred's life, the above-mentioned army of heathen passed
through Mercia into East Anglia, and wintered at Thetford.[3]

33. The Danes triumph.[2] — That same year Edmund,
King of the East Angles, fought most fiercely against that
army; but, lamentable to say, the heathen triumphed,
for he and most of his men were there slain, while the
enemy held the battle-field, and reduced all that region to
subjection.

34. Ceolnoth dies.[4] — That same year Ceolnoth, Archbishop of Canterbury, went the way of all flesh, and was
buried in peace in that city.

---

[1] Here and elsewhere in the text often spelled Æthered.
[2] From the *Chronicle*.   [3] In Norfolk.
[4] Mostly from the *Chronicle*.

35. The Danes defeated at Englefield.[1] — In the year of our Lord's incarnation 871, which was the twenty-third of King Alfred's life, the heathen army, of hateful memory, left East Anglia, and, entering the kingdom of the West Saxons, came to the royal vill called Reading, situated on the south bank of the Thames, in the district called Berkshire; and there, on the third day after their arrival, their <two> ealdormen, with great part of the army, rode forth for plunder, while the others made an entrenchment between the rivers Thames and Kennet, on the southern side of the same royal vill. They were encountered by Æthelwulf, Ealdorman of Berkshire, with his men, at a place called Englefield[2] <in English, and in Latin 'The Field of the Angles'>.[3] Both sides fought bravely, and made long resistance to each other. At length one of the heathen ealdormen was slain, and the greater part of the army destroyed; upon which the rest saved themselves by flight, and the Christians gained the victory and held the battle-field.

36. Battle of Reading.[1] — Four days afterwards, King Æthelred and his brother Alfred, uniting their forces and assembling an army, marched to Reading, where, on their arrival at the castle gate, they cut to pieces and overthrew the heathen whom they found outside the fortifications. But the heathen fought no less valiantly and, rushing like wolves out of every gate, waged battle with all their might. Both sides fought long and fiercely, but at last, sad to say, the Christians turned their backs, the heathen obtained the victory and held the battle-field, the aforesaid Ealdorman Æthelwulf being among the slain.

---

[1] Chiefly from the *Chronicle*.
[2] Five and one-half miles southwest of Reading.
[3] Added from Florence of Worcester by Stevenson.

37. Battle of Ashdown.[1] — Roused by this grief and shame, the Christians, after four days, with all their forces and much spirit advanced to battle against the aforesaid army, at a place called Ashdown,[2] which in Latin signifies 'Ash's[3] Hill.' The heathen, forming in two divisions, arranged two shield-walls of similar size; and since they had two kings and many ealdormen, they gave the middle[4] part of the army to the two kings, and the other part to all the ealdormen. The Christians, perceiving this, divided their army also into two troops, and with no less zeal formed shield-walls.[5] But Alfred, as I have been told by truthful eye-witnesses, marched up swiftly with his men to the battle-field; for King Æthelred had remained a long time in his tent in prayer, hearing mass, and declaring that he would not depart thence alive till the priest had done, and that he was not disposed to abandon the service of God for that of men; and according to these sentiments he acted. This faith of the Christian king availed much with the Lord, as I shall show more fully in the sequel.

38. Alfred begins the Attack.[6] — Now the Christians had determined that King Æthelred, with his men, should attack the two heathen kings, and that his brother Alfred, with his troops, should take the chance of war against all the leaders of the heathen. Things being so arranged on

---

[1] Chiefly from the *Chronicle*.

[2] The Berkshire Downs (Stevenson).

[3] Stevenson is convinced that Æscesdun, though interpreted as 'mons fraxini,' cannot mean 'the hill of the ash,' but that Ash is here a man's name.

[4] Perhaps *mediam* is a scribal error for *unam* or *primam* (Stevenson).

[5] There is a note on the Germanic shield-wall in my edition of *Judith* (305[a]), in the Belles Lettres Series.

[6] All original except final clause.

both sides, the king still continued a long time in prayer, and the heathen, prepared for battle, had hastened to the field. Then Alfred, though only second in command, could no longer support the advance of the enemy, unless he either retreated or charged upon them without waiting for his brother. At length, with the rush of a wild boar, he courageously led the Christian troops against the hostile army, as he had already designed, for, although the king had not yet arrived, he relied upon God's counsel and trusted to His aid. Hence, having closed up his shield-wall in due order, he straightway advanced his standards against the foe. <At length King Æthelred, having finished the prayers in which he was engaged, came up, and, having invoked the King of the universe, entered upon the engagement.>[1]

39. The Heathen Rout and Loss.[2] — But here I must inform those who are ignorant of the fact that the field of battle was not equally advantageous to both parties, since the heathen had seized the higher ground, and the Christian array was advancing up-hill. In that place there was a solitary low thorn-tree, which I have seen with my own eyes, and round this the opposing forces met in strife with deafening uproar from all, the one side bent on evil, the other on fighting for life, and dear ones, and fatherland. When both armies had fought bravely and fiercely for a long while, the heathen, being unable by God's decree longer to endure the onset of the Christians, the larger part of their force being slain, betook themselves to shameful flight. There fell one of the two heathen kings and five ealdormen; many thousand of their men were either slain at this spot or lay scattered far and wide over the

---

[1] Supplied by Stevenson from Florence of Worcester.
[2] Mostly original.

whole field of Ashdown. Thus there fell King Bagsecg, Ealdorman Sidroc the Elder and Ealdorman Sidroc the Younger, Ealdorman Osbern, Ealdorman Fræna, and Ealdorman Harold; and the whole heathen army pursued its flight, not only until night, but until the next day, even until they reached the stronghold[1] from which they had sallied. The Christians followed, slaying all they could reach, until it became dark.

40. Battle of Basing.[2] — After[3] fourteen days had elapsed King Æthelred and his brother Alfred joined their forces, and marched to Basing[4] to fight with the heathen. Having thus assembled, battle was joined, and they held their own for a long time, but the heathen gained the victory, and held possession of the battle-field. After this fight, another army of heathen came from beyond sea, and joined them.

41. Æthelred's Death.[5] — That same year, after Easter, the aforesaid King Æthelred, having bravely, honorably, and with good repute governed his kingdom five years through many tribulations, went the way of all flesh, and was buried in Wimborne Minster,[6] where he awaits the coming of the Lord and the first resurrection with the just.

42. Alfred comes to the Throne; Battle of Wilton.[7] — That same year the aforesaid Alfred, who had been up to that time, during the lifetime of his brothers, only of secondary rank, now, on the death of his brother, by God's permission undertook the government of the whole

---

[1] Probably Reading.   [2] From the *Chronicle*.

[3] Before this sentence occurs the following in the Latin: *Quibus cum talia præsentis vitæ dispendia alienigenis perperam quærentibus non sufficerent.* This may represent a sentence in the author's draft that was intended, owing to change of construction, to be omitted (Stevenson).   [4] In Hampshire.

[5] Mostly from the *Chronicle*.   [6] In Dorsetshire.

[7] Paraphrased and amplified from the *Chronicle*.

kingdom, amid the acclamations of all the people; and
indeed, if he had chosen, he might easily have done so with
the general consent whilst his brother above named was
still alive, since in wisdom and every other good quality he
surpassed all his brothers, and especially because he was
brave and victorious in nearly every battle. And when he
had reigned a month almost against his will — for he did not
think that he alone, without divine aid, could sustain the
ferocity of the heathen, though even during his brothers'
lifetimes he had borne the calamities of many — he fought
a fierce battle with a few men, and on very unequal terms,
against all the army of the heathen, at a hill called Wilton,
on the south bank of the river Wiley,[1] from which river
the whole of that shire is named; and after a severe
engagement, lasting a considerable part of the day, the
heathen, seeing the whole extent of the danger they were
in, and no longer able to bear the attack of their enemies,
turned their backs and fled. But, shame to say, they
took advantage of their pursuers' rashness,[2] and, again
rallying, gained the victory and kept the battle-field. Let
no one be surprised that the Christians had but a small
number of men, for the Saxons as a people had been all
but worn out by eight battles in this selfsame year against
the heathen, in which there died one king, nine chieftains,
and innumerable troops of soldiers, not to speak of countless skirmishes both by night and by day, in which the oft-
named <King> Alfred, and all the leaders of that people, with
their men, and many of the king's thanes, had been engaged
in unwearied strife against the heathen. How many thousand heathen fell in these numberless skirmishes God alone

[1] A tributary of the Nadder, which it joins near Wilton.
[2] Or, perhaps, 'fewness,' reading *paucitatem* for *peraudacitatem*
(Stevenson).

knows, over and above those who were slain in the eight battles above mentioned.

43. Peace made.[1] — In that same year the Saxons made peace with the heathen, on condition that they should take their departure; and this they did.

44. The Heathen winter in London.[2] — In the year of our Lord's incarnation 872, being the twenty-fourth of King Alfred's life, the aforesaid army of heathen went to London, and there wintered; and the Mercians made peace with them.

45. The Heathen winter in Lindsey.[2] — In the year of our Lord's incarnation 873, being the twenty-fifth of King Alfred's life, the oft-named army, leaving London, went into Northumbria, and there wintered in the shire of Lindsey; and the Mercians again made peace with them.

46. The Danes in Mercia.[3] — In the year of our Lord's incarnation 874, being the twenty-sixth of King Alfred's life, the above-named army left Lindsey and marched to Mercia, where they wintered at Repton.[4] Also they compelled Burgred, King of Mercia, against his will to leave his kingdom and go beyond sea to Rome, in the twenty-second year of his reign. He did not live long after his arrival at Rome, but died there, and was honorably buried in the Colony of the Saxons,[5] in St. Mary's church,[6] where he awaits the Lord's coming and the first resurrection with the just. The heathen also, after his expulsion, subjected the whole kingdom of Mercia to their dominion; but, by a miserable arrangement, gave it into the custody of a certain foolish

---

[1] Mostly from the *Chronicle*.   [2] From the *Chronicle*.
[3] Chiefly from the *Chronicle*.   [4] In Derbyshire.
[5] Among the Germans there were Colonies (*Scholæ*) of the Frisians, Franks, and Lombards, as well as of the Saxons.
[6] Now Santo Spirito in Sassia, near the Vatican.

man, named Ceolwulf, one of the <king's> thanes, on condition that he should peaceably restore it to them on what-
soever day they should wish to have it again; and to bind
this agreement he gave them hostages, and swore that he
would not oppose their will in any way, but be obedient to
them in every respect.

47. The Danes in Northumbria and Cambridge.[1] — In the year
of our Lord's incarnation 875, being the twenty-seventh of
King Alfred's life, the above-mentioned army, leaving
Repton, separated into two bodies, one of which went with
Halfdene into Northumbria, and having wintered there
near the Tyne, and reduced all Northumbria to subjection,
also ravaged the Picts and the people of Strathclyde.[2]
The other division, with Guthrum,[3] Oscytel, and Anwind,
three kings of the heathen, went to Cambridge, and there
wintered.

48. Alfred's Battle at Sea.[4] — In that same year King
Alfred fought a battle at sea against six ships of the heathen,
and took one of them, the rest escaping by flight.

49. Movements of the Danes.[5] — In the year of our Lord's
incarnation 876, being the twenty-eighth year of King
Alfred's life, the oft-mentioned army of the heathen, leaving Cambridge by night, entered a fortress called Wareham,[6]
where there is a monastery of nuns between the two rivers
Froom <and Tarrant>, in the district which is called in Welsh
Durngueir,[7] but in Saxon Thornsæta,[8] placed in a most
secure location, except on the western side, where there was
a territory adjacent. With this army Alfred made a solemn
treaty to the effect that they should depart from him, and

---

[1] From the *Chronicle*.
[2] The valley of the Clyde.
[3] Here spelled Gothrum.
[4] From the *Chronicle*.
[5] Chiefly from the *Chronicle*.
[6] In Dorsetshire.
[7] Dorchester.
[8] For the usual Dornsæte.

they made no hesitation to give him as many picked hostages as he named; also they swore an oath on all the relics in which King Alfred trusted next to God,[1] and on which they had never before sworn to any people, that they would speedily depart from his kingdom. But they again practised their usual treachery, and caring nothing for either hostages or oath, they broke the treaty, and, sallying forth by night, slew all the horsemen [horses ?] that they had,[2] and, turning off, started without warning for another place called in Saxon Exanceastre, and in Welsh Cairwisc, which means in Latin 'The City <of Exe>,' situated on the eastern bank of the river Wise,[3] near the southern sea which divides Britain from Gaul, and there passed the winter.

50. Halfdene partitions Northumbria. — In that same year Halfdene, king of that part of Northumbria, divided up the whole region between himself and his men, and settled there with his army.

51. Division of Mercia.[4] — The same year, in the month of August, that army went into Mercia, and gave part of the district of the Mercians to one Ceolwulf,[5] a weak-minded thane of the king; the rest they divided among themselves.

52. The Danes at Chippenham.[6] — In the year of our Lord's incarnation 878, being the thirtieth of King Alfred's life, the oft-mentioned army left Exeter, and went to Chippenham, a royal vill, situated in the north of Wiltshire, on the east bank of the river which is called Avon in Welsh, and

---

[1] Here the *Chronicle* has 'on the holy arm-ring,' on which the Danes, it would seem, were accustomed to swear.

[2] Here the *Chronicle* has: 'They, the mounted army, stole away from the *fierd* [the English forces] in the night into Exeter.' This, of course, is the true account, while the statement in Asser is incredible.

[3] Exe.

[4] From the *Chronicle*.

[5] See chap. 46.

[6] Largely from the *Chronicle*.

there wintered. And they drove many of that people by
their arms, by poverty, and by fear, to voyage beyond sea,
and reduced almost all the inhabitants of that district to
subjection.

53. Alfred in Somersetshire. — At that same time the
above-mentioned King Alfred, with a few of his nobles, and
certain soldiers and vassals, was leading in great tribulation an unquiet life among the woodlands and swamps of
Somersetshire; for he had nothing that he needed except
what by frequent sallies he could forage openly or stealthily
from the heathen or from the Christians who had submitted
to the rule of the heathen.[1]

54. The Danes defeated at Cynwit.[2] — In that same year
the brother[3] of Inwar[4] and Halfdene, with twenty-three
ships, came, after many massacres of the Christians, from
Dyfed,[5] where he had wintered, and sailed to Devon, where
with twelve hundred others he met with a miserable death,
being slain, while committing his misdeeds, by the king's
thanes, before the fortress of Cynwit,[6] in which many of
the king's thanes, with their followers, had shut themselves
up for safety. The heathen, seeing that the fortress was
unprepared and altogether unfortified, except that it merely
had fortifications after our manner, determined not to
assault it, because that place is rendered secure by its position on all sides except the eastern, as I myself have seen,
but began to besiege it, thinking that those men would
soon surrender from famine, thirst, and the blockade, since

[1] At this point Archbishop Parker interpolated, from the *Annals
of St. Neots*, the story of Alfred and the cakes. This story, however,
cannot be proved to antedate the Norman Conquest.

[2] The first clause from the *Chronicle;* the rest original.

[3] Name unknown.   [5] Or South Wales. See chap. 80.

[4] Hingwar.   [6] Site unknown.

there is no water close to the fortress. But the result did not fall out as they expected; for the Christians, before they began at all to suffer from such want, being inspired by Heaven, and judging it much better to gain either victory or death, sallied out suddenly upon the heathen at daybreak, and from the first cut them down in great numbers, slaying also their king, so that few escaped to their ships.

55. Alfred at Athelney.[1] — The same year, after Easter, King Alfred, with a few men, made a stronghold in a place called Athelney,[2] and from thence sallied with his vassals of Somerset to make frequent and unwearied assaults upon the heathen. And again, the seventh week after Easter, he rode to Egbert's Stone,[3] which is in the eastern part of Selwood Forest (in Latin 'Great Forest,' and in Welsh Coit Maur). Here he was met by all the neighboring folk of Somersetshire and Wiltshire, and such of Hampshire as had not sailed beyond sea for fear of the heathen; and when they saw the king restored alive, as it were, after such great tribulation, they were filled, as was meet, with immeasurable joy, and encamped there for one night. At daybreak of the following morning, the king struck his camp, and came to Æglea,[4] where he encamped for one night.

56. Battle of Edington, and Treaty with Guthrum.[5] — The next morning at dawn he moved his standards to Edington,[6] and there fought bravely and perseveringly by means of a close shield-wall against the whole army of the heathen,

---

[1] Mostly from the *Chronicle*.
[2] In Somersetshire.   [3] Unknown.
[4] Or perhaps better, Iglea; see Stevenson's note on the word, p. 270 of his edition. He says: 'It is probably an older name of Southleigh Wood, or of part of it.'
[5] Based upon the *Chronicle*.   [6] In Wiltshire.

whom at length, with the divine help, he defeated with
great slaughter, and pursued them flying to their stronghold. Immediately he slew all the men and carried off all
the horses and cattle that he could find without the fortress,
and thereupon pitched his camp, with all his army, before
the gates of the heathen stronghold. And when he had
remained there fourteen days, the heathen, terrified by
hunger, cold, fear, and last of all by despair, begged for
peace, engaging to give the king as many designated hostages as he pleased, and to receive none from him in return
— in which manner they had never before made peace
with any one. The king, hearing this embassage, of his
own motion took pity upon them, and received from them
the designated hostages, as many as he would. Thereupon
the heathen swore, besides, that they would straightway
leave his kingdom; and their king, Guthrum, promised to
embrace Christianity, and receive baptism at King Alfred's
hands — all of which articles he and his men fulfilled as
they had promised. For after <three>[1] weeks Guthrum, king
of the heathen, with thirty[2] men chosen from his army,
came to Alfred at a place called Aller, near Athelney, and
there King Alfred, receiving him as a son by adoption,
raised him up from the holy font of baptism. On the eighth
day, at a royal vill named Wedmore, his chrism-loosing[3]

---

[1] Supplied by Stevenson from the *Chronicle*.

[2] Properly, as one of thirty, according to the *Chronicle*.

[3] Chrism is the term employed for the mixture of oil and balsam
employed in the rite of confirmation, and sometimes for the ceremony
of confirmation itself. In the early church, this ceremony immediately
followed baptism, and was performed by the laying on of hands. In
the Roman church it is obligatory on all Catholics, and no baptism is
theoretically complete without it. It is performed by a bishop (only
exceptionally by a priest). The ceremony begins with the bishop's rising and facing the person or persons to be confirmed, his pastoral staff

took place. After his baptism he remained twelve days with the king, who, together with all his companions, gave him many rich gifts.[1]

57. The Danes go to Cirencester.[2] — In the year of our Lord's incarnation 879, which was the thirty-first of King Alfred's life, the aforesaid army of heathen, leaving Chippenham, as they had promised, went to Cirencester, which is called in Welsh Cairceri, and is situated in the southern

in his hand, and saying: 'May the Holy Ghost come upon you, and the power of the Holy Ghost keep you from sins '(*Handbook to Christian and Ecclesiastical Rome: Liturgy in Rome*, London, 1897, pp. 169-171). The rite is described in Egbert's *Pontifical*, which may be taken as representing the custom in the church of Alfred's time. Lingard says (*Anglo-Saxon Church*, London, 1858, 1. 297): 'According to that pontifical, the bishop prayed thus: "Almighty and Everlasting God, who hast granted to this thy servant to be born again of water and the Holy Ghost, and hast given to him remission of his sins, send down upon him thy sevenfold Holy Spirit, the Paraclete from heaven, Amen. Give to him the spirit of wisdom and understanding, Amen — the spirit of counsel and fortitude, Amen — the spirit of knowledge and piety, Amen. Fill him with the spirit of the fear of God and our Lord Jesus Christ, and mercifully sign him with the sign of the holy cross for life eternal." The bishop then marked his forehead with chrism, and proceeded thus: "Receive this sign of the holy cross with the chrism of salvation in Christ Jesus unto life eternal." The head was then bound with a fillet of new linen to be worn seven days, and the bishop resumed: "O God, who didst give thy Holy Spirit to thine apostles, that by them and their successors he might be given to the rest of the faithful, look down on the ministry of our lowliness, and grant that into the heart of him whose forehead we have this day anointed, and confirmed with the sign of the cross, thy Holy Spirit may descend; and that, dwelling therein, he may make it the temple of his glory, through Christ our Lord." The confirmed then received the episcopal blessing, and communicated during the mass.'

The chrism-loosing was the ceremony of unbinding the fillet, apparently.

[1] MS. *ædificia;* Stevenson, *beneficia.*   [2] Chiefly from the *Chronicle.*

part of the kingdom of the Hwicce,[1] and there they remained one year.

58. Danes at Fulham.[2] — In that same year a large army of heathen sailed from beyond sea into the river Thames, and joined the greater army. However, they wintered at Fulham, near the river Thames.

59. An Eclipse.[3] — In that same year an eclipse[4] of the sun took place between nones and vespers, but nearer to nones.

60. The Danes in East Anglia.[5] — In the year of our Lord's incarnation 880, which was the thirty-second of King Alfred's life, the oft-mentioned army of heathen left Ciren-cester, and went to East Anglia, where they divided up the country and began to settle.

61. The Smaller Army leaves England.[6] — That same year the army of heathen, which had wintered at Fulham, left the island of Britain, and sailed over sea to East Frankland, where they remained for a year at a place called Ghent.

62. The Danes fight with the Franks. — In the year of our Lord's incarnation 881, which was the thirty-third of King Alfred's life, the army went further on into Frankland, and the Franks fought against them; and after the battle the heathen, obtaining horses, became an army of cavalry.

63. The Danes on the Meuse.[7] — In the year of our Lord's incarnation 882, which was the thirty-fourth of King Alfred's life, the aforesaid army sailed their ships up into Frankland by a river called the Meuse, and there wintered one year.

64. Alfred's Naval Battle with the Danes.[8] — In that same year Alfred, King of the Anglo-Saxons, fought a battle at

---

[1] Gloucester, Worcester, etc.
[2] Mostly from the *Chronicle*.
[3] Mostly from the *Chronicle*.
[4] See Stevenson's interesting note.
[5] From the *Chronicle*.
[6] *Ibid.*
[7] *Ibid.*
[8] *Ibid.*

sea against the heathen fleet, of which he captured two ships, and slew all who were on board. Two commanders of the other ships, with all their crews, worn out by the fight and their wounds, laid down their arms, and submitted to the king on bended knees with many entreaties.

65. The Danes at Condé.[1] — In the year of our Lord's incarnation 883, which was the thirty-fifth of King Alfred's life, the aforesaid army sailed their ships up the river called Scheldt to a convent of nuns called Condé, and there remained one year.

66. Deliverance of Rochester.[2] — In the year of our Lord's incarnation 884, which was the thirty-sixth of King Alfred's life, the aforesaid army divided into two parts: one body of them went into East Frankland, and the other, coming to Britain, entered Kent, where they besieged a city called in Saxon Rochester, situated on the east bank of the river Medway. Before the gate of the town the heathen suddenly erected a strong fortress; but they were unable to take the city, because the citizens defended themselves bravely until King Alfred came up to help them with a large army. Then the heathen abandoned their fortress and all the horses which they had brought with them out of Frankland, and, leaving behind them in the fortress the greater part of their prisoners on the sudden arrival of the king, fled in haste to their ships; the Saxons immediately seized upon the prisoners and horses left by the heathen; and so the latter, compelled by dire necessity, returned the same summer to Frankland.

67. Alfred's Naval Battle at the Mouth of the Stour.[3] — In that same year Alfred, King of the Anglo-Saxons, shifted his fleet, full of fighting men, from Kent to East

---

[1] Mostly from the *Chronicle*.   [2] Largely from the *Chronicle*.
[3] Mostly from the *Chronicle*.

Anglia,[1] for the sake of spoil. No sooner had they arrived
at the mouth of the river Stour than thirteen ships of
the heathen met them, prepared for battle; a fierce naval
combat ensued, and the heathen were all slain; all the
ships, with all their money, were taken. After this, while
the victorious royal fleet was reposing,[2] the heathen who
occupied East Anglia assembled their ships from every
quarter, met the same royal fleet at sea in the mouth of the
same river, and, after a naval engagement, gained the
victory.

68. Death of Carloman, of Louis II, and of Louis III.[3] —
In that same year also, Carloman, King of the West
Franks, while engaged in a boar-hunt, was miserably slain
by a boar, which inflicted a dreadful wound on him with
its tusk. His brother Louis, who had also been King of the
Franks, had died the year before. Both these were sons of
Louis,[4] King of the Franks, who also had died in the year
above mentioned, in which the eclipse of the sun took
place.[5] This Louis was the son of Charles,[6] King of the
Franks, whose daughter Judith[7] Æthelwulf, King of the
West Saxons, took to queen with her father's consent.

69. The Danes in Old Saxony.[8] — In that same year a
great army of the heathen came from Germany[9] into the
country of the Old Saxons, which is called in Saxon Eald-
Seaxum. To oppose them the same Saxons and Frisians
joined their forces, and fought bravely twice in that same

[1] Cf. chap. 60.
[2] The MS. has *dormiret*, but perhaps for *domum iret*, since the
Chronicle has *hāmweard wendon* (Stevenson); so perhaps we should
read 'was on its way home.'
[3] Chiefly from the *Chronicle*.   [6] Charles the Bald.
[4] Louis the Stammerer.   [7] Cf. chaps. 11 and 13,
[5] Cf. chap. 59.   [8] From the *Chronicle*.
[9] From Duisburg, about January, 884 (Stevenson).

year.[1] In both these battles the Christians, by God's merciful aid, gained the victory.

70. Charles, King of the Alemanni.[2] — In that same year also, Charles, King of the Alemanni, received with universal consent the kingdom of the West Franks, and all the kingdoms which lie between the Tyrrhene Sea and that gulf[3] situated between the Old Saxons and the Gauls, with the exception of the kingdom of Armorica.[4] This Charles was the son of King Louis,[5] who was brother of Charles, King of the Franks, father of Judith, the aforesaid queen; these two brothers were sons of Louis,[6] Louis being the son of Charlemagne, son of Pepin.

71. Death of Pope Marinus.[7] — In that same year Pope Marinus, of blessed memory, went the way of all flesh; it was he who, for the love of Alfred, King of the Anglo-Saxons, and at his request, generously freed the Saxon Colony in Rome from all tribute and tax. He also sent to the aforesaid king many gifts on that occasion, among which was no small portion of the most holy and venerable cross on which our Lord Jesus Christ hung for the salvation of all mankind.

72. The Danes break their Treaty.[8] — In that same year also the army of heathen which dwelt in East Anglia disgracefully broke the peace which they had concluded with King Alfred.

73. Asser makes a New Beginning.[9] — And now, to return to that from which I digressed, lest I be compelled by my

[1] There was a battle in Frisia, about December, 884, and a later one in Saxony (Stevenson).
[2] Mainly from the *Chronicle*.
[3] The North Sea.
[4] Brittany.
[5] Louis the German.
[6] Louis the Pious.
[7] Mainly from the *Chronicle*.
[8] From the *Chronicle*.
[9] Based upon the preface to Eginhard's *Life of Charlemagne*.

long navigation to abandon the haven, of desired rest,[1] I
propose, as far as my knowledge will enable me, to speak
somewhat concerning the life, character, and just conduct,
and in no small degree concerning the deeds, of my lord
Alfred, King of the Anglo-Saxons, after he married the
said respected wife of noble Mercian race; and, with God's
blessing, I will despatch it concisely and briefly, as I promised, that I may not, by prolixity in relating each new
event, offend the minds of those who may be somewhat
hard to please.

74. Alfred's Maladies.[2] — While his nuptials were being
honorably celebrated in Mercia, among innumerable multi-
tudes of both sexes, and after long feasts by night and by day,
he was suddenly seized, in the presence of all the people, by
instant and overwhelming pain, unknown to any physician.
No one there knew, nor even those who daily see him up
to the present time — and this, sad to say, is the worst of
all, that it should have continued uninterruptedly through
the revolutions of so many years, from the twentieth to the
fortieth year of his life and more — whence such a malady
arose. Many thought that it was occasioned by the favor
and fascination of the people who surrounded him; others,
by some spite of the devil, who is ever jealous of good men;
others, from an unusual kind of fever; while still others
thought it was the *ficus*,[3] which species of severe disease
he had had from his childhood. On a certain occasion it
had come to pass by the divine will that when he had
gone to Cornwall on a hunting expedition, and had turned
out of the road to pray in a certain church in which rests
Saint Gueriir [and now also St. Neot reposes there],[4] he
had of his own accord prostrated himself for a long time

[1] See chap. 21.   [2] Original.   [3] Perhaps the hemorrhoids.
[4] Interpolated some time between 893 and 1000 A.D.

in silent prayer — since from childhood he had been a frequent visitor of holy places for prayer and the giving of
alms — and there he besought the mercy of the Lord that,
in his boundless clemency, Almighty God would exchange
the torments of the malady which then afflicted him for
some other lighter disease, provided that such disease
should not show itself outwardly in his body, lest he should
be useless and despised — for he had great dread of leprosy
or blindness, or any such complaint as instantly makes
men useless and despised at its coming. When he had
finished his praying, he proceeded on his journey, and not
long after felt within himself that he had been divinely
healed, according to his request, of that disorder, and that
it was entirely eradicated, although he had obtained even
this complaint in the first flower of his youth by his devout
and frequent prayers and supplications to God. For if I
may be allowed to speak concisely, though in a somewhat
inverted order, of his zealous piety to God — in his earliest
youth, before he married his wife, he wished to establish
his mind in God's commandments, for he perceived that he
could not abstain from carnal desires[1]; and because he
saw that he should incur the anger of God if he did anything contrary to His will, he used often to rise at cockcrow and at the matin hours, and go to pray in churches
and at the relics of the saints. There he would prostrate
himself, and pray that Almighty God in His mercy would
strengthen his mind still more in the love of His service,
converting it fully to Himself by some infirmity such as he
might bear, but not such as would render him contempt-
ible and useless in worldly affairs. Now when he had

---

[1] In Alfred's prayer at the end of his translation of Boethius, one
of the petitions is: 'Deliver me from foul lust and from all unright-
eousness.'

often prayed with much devotion to this effect, after an
interval of some time he incurred as a gift from God the
before-named disease of the *ficus*, which he bore long and
painfully for many years, even despairing of life, until he
entirely got rid of it by prayer. But, sad to say, though
it had been removed, a worse one seized him, as I have
said, at his marriage, and this incessantly tormented him,
night and day, from the twentieth to the forty-fifth year of
his life. But if ever, by God's mercy, he was relieved from
this infirmity for a single day or night, or even for the
space of one hour, yet the fear and dread of that terrible
malady never left him, but rendered him almost useless, as
he thought, in every affair, whether human or divine.

   75. Alfred's Children and their Education.[1] — The sons and
daughters whom he had by his wife above-mentioned were
Æthelflæd, the eldest, after whom came Edward, then
Æthelgivu, then Ælfthryth, and finally Æthelward —
besides those who died in childhood. The number of . . .[2]
Æthelflaed, when she arrived at a marriageable age, was
united to Æthelred,[3] Ealdorman of Mercia. Æthelgivu,
having dedicated her maidenhood to God, entered His service, and submitted to the rules of the monastic life, to
which she was consecrate. Æthelward, the youngest, by
the divine counsel and by the admirable foresight of the
king, was intrusted to the schools of literary training,
where, with the children of almost all the nobility of the
country, and many also who were not noble, he was under
the diligent care of the teachers. Books in both languages,
namely, Latin and Saxon, were diligently read in the
school.[4] They also learned to write; so that before they

---

[1] Original.
[2] This is the beginning of a corrupt sentence, of which nothing has
been made.   [3] MS. *Eadredo*.   [4] See Appendix I, p. 70.

were of an age to practise human arts, namely, hunting
and other pursuits which befit noblemen, they became
studious and clever in the liberal arts. Edward and Ælfthryth were always bred up in the king's court, and received
great attention from their tutors and nurses; nay, they
continue to this day, with much love from every one, to
show humbleness, affability, and gentleness towards all,
both natives and foreigners, while remaining in complete
subjection to their father. Nor, among the other pursuits
which appertain to this life and are fit for noble youths,
are they suffered to pass their time idly and unprofitably
without liberal training; for they have carefully learned
the Psalms[1] and Saxon books, especially Saxon poems, and
are in the habit of making frequent use of books.

76. Alfred's Varied Pursuits.[2] — In the meantime, the king,
during the wars and frequent trammels of this present
life, the invasions of the heathen, and his own daily infirmities of body, continued to carry on the government, and
to practise hunting in all its branches; to teach his gold-
smiths[3] and all his artificers, his falconers, hawkers, and
dog-keepers; to build houses, majestic and rich beyond all
custom of his predecessors, after his own new designs; to
recite the Saxon books, and especially to learn by heart
Saxon poems,[4] and to make others learn them, he alone
never ceasing from studying most diligently to the best of
his ability. He daily attended mass and the other services
of religion; recited certain psalms, together with prayers,
and the daily and nightly hour-service; and frequented the
churches at night, as I have said, that he might pray in

---

[1] See chaps. 24 and 88.
[2] Original.
[3] Cf . Alfred's jewel, and the book upon it by Professor Earle.
[4] See chaps. 23 and 75.

secret, apart from others. He bestowed alms and largesses both on natives and on foreigners of all countries; was most affable and agreeable to all; and was skilful in the investigation of things unknown.[1] Many Franks, Frisians,[2] Gauls, heathen,[3] Welsh, Irish,[4] and Bretons,[5] noble and simple, submitted voluntarily to his dominion; and all of them, according to their worthiness,[6] he ruled, loved, honored, and enriched with money and power, as if they had been his own people.[7] Moreover, he was sedulous and zealous in the habit of hearing the divine Scriptures read by his own countrymen, or if, by any chance it so happened that any one arrived from abroad, to hear prayers in company with foreigners. His bishops, too, and all the clergy, his ealdormen and nobles, his personal attendants and friends, he loved with wonderful affection. Their sons, too, who were bred up in the royal household, were no less dear to him than his own; he never ceased to instruct them in all kinds of good morals, and, among other things, himself to teach them literature night and day. But as if he had no consolation in all these things, and suffered no other annoyance either from within or without, he was so

---

[1] Our first accounts of Arctic exploration are from his pen. For his interest in geographical discovery see the narratives of Ohthere and Wulfstan, in his translation of Orosius. In 897, according to the *Chronicle*, he was experimenting with new war-galleys: 'They were almost twice as long as the others. Some had sixty oars, some more. They were swifter, steadier, and higher than the others, and were built, not on a Frisian or Danish model, but according to his personal notions of their utility.'

[2] There were Frisians in his fleet in 897 (*Chronicle*).

[3] Northmen; such were Ohthere and Wulfstan (see note 1, above).

[4] Three such came to him in 891 (*Chronicle*).

[5] MS. *Armorici*. See chap. 102.

[6] Or, 'degrees'; cf. p. 60.   [7] See chap. 101.

harassed by daily and nightly sadness that he complained
and made moan to the Lord, and to all who were admitted
to his familiarity and affection, that Almighty God had
made him ignorant of divine wisdom and of the liberal
arts; in this emulating the pious, famous, and wealthy
Solomon, King of the Hebrews, who at the outset, despising all present glory and riches, asked wisdom of God, and
yet found both, namely, wisdom and present glory; as it
is written, 'Seek first the kingdom of God and his righteous-
ness, and all these things shall be added unto you.'[1] But
God, who is always the observer of the thoughts of the
inward mind, the instigator of meditations and of all good
purposes, and a plentiful aider in the formation of good
desires — for He would never inspire a man to aim at the
good unless He also amply supplied that which the man
justly and properly wished to have — stirred up the king's
mind from within, not from without; as it is written, 'I
will hearken what the Lord God will say concerning me.'[2]
He would avail himself of every opportunity to procure
assistants in his good designs, to aid him in his strivings
after wisdom, that he might attain to what he aimed at;
and, like a prudent bee,[3] which, rising in summer at early
morning from her beloved cells, steers her course with
rapid flight along the uncertain paths of the air, and
descends on the manifold and varied flowers of grasses,
herbs, and shrubs, essaying that which most pleases her,
and bearing it home, he directed the eyes of his mind afar,
and sought that without which he had not within, that is,
in his own kingdom.[4]

[1] Matt. 6. 33.   [2] Ps. 85. 8.
[3] Cf . chap. 88; Stevenson gives a number of parallels from ancient
and mediæval authors, beginning with Lucretius (3. 9) and Seneca
(*Epist.* 84.3).   [4] Cf. chap. 24.

77. Alfred's Scholarly Associates: Werfrith, Plegmund, Æthelstan, and Werwulf.[1]

— But God at that time, as some consolation to the king's benevolence, enduring no longer his kindly and just complaint, sent as it were certain luminaries, namely, Werfrith,[2] Bishop of the church of Worcester, a man well versed in divine Scripture, who, by the king's command, was the first to interpret with clearness and elegance the books of the *Dialogues* of Pope Gregory and Peter, his disciple, from Latin into Saxon, sometimes putting sense for sense; then Plegmund,[3] a Mercian by birth. Archbishop of the church of Canterbury, a venerable man, endowed with wisdom; besides Æthelstan[4] and Werwulf, learned priests and clerks,[5] Mercians by birth. These four King Alfred had called to him from Mercia, and he exalted them with many honors and powers in the kingdom of the West Saxons, not to speak of those which Archbishop Plegmund and Bishop Werfrith had in Mercia. By the teaching and wisdom of all these the king's desire increased continually, and was gratified. Night and day, whenever he had any leisure, he commanded such men as these to read books to him — for he never suffered himself to be without one of them — so that he came to possess a knowledge of almost every book, though of himself he could not yet understand anything of books, since he had not yet learned to read anything.

[1] Original.

[2] See Appendix I, p. 69. In Alfred's will he gives Werfrith (Wærferth) a hundred marks.

[3] See Appendix I, p. 71.

[4] Perhaps Bishop of Ramsbury (909 A.D.). The later MSS. of the *Chronicle* say, under the year 883: 'And in the same year Sighelm and Æthelstan took to Rome the alms that King Alfred sent, and also to India to St. Thomas' and St. Bartholomew's.'

[5] Or, 'chaplains.' See p. 61, note 6.

78. Grimbald and John, the Old Saxon.[1] — But since the king's commendable avarice could not be gratified even in this, he sent messengers beyond sea to Gaul, to procure teachers, and invited from thence Grimbald,[2] priest and monk, a venerable man and excellent singer, learned in every kind of ecclesiastical discipline and in holy Scripture, and adorned with all virtues. He also obtained from thence John,[3] both priest and monk, a man of the keenest intellect, learned in all branches of literature, and skilled in many other arts. By the teaching of these men the king's mind was greatly enlarged, and he enriched and honored them with much power.

79. Asset's Negotiations with King Alfred.[4] — At that time I also came to Wessex, out of the furthest coasts of Western Wales; and when I had proposed to go to him through many intervening provinces, I arrived in the country of the South Saxons, which in Saxon is called Sussex, under the guidance of some of that nation; and there I first saw him in the royal vill which is called Dene.[5] He received me with kindness, and, among other conversation, besought me eagerly to devote myself to his service and become his friend, and to leave for his sake everything which I possessed on the northern and western side of the Severn, promising he would give me more than an equivalent for it, as in fact he did. I replied that I could not incautiously and rashly promise such things; for it seemed to me unjust that I should leave those sacred places in which I had been

---

[1] Original.

[2] Probably from the monastery of St. Bertin, at St. Omer (Pas-de- . Calais). See Appendix I, p. 71, and Appendix II, pp. 75ff.

[3] Cf. chap. 94, and Appendix I, p. 71.

[4] Original.

[5] Perhaps Dean, near Eastbourne, in Sussex.

bred and educated, where I had received the tonsure, and
had at length been ordained, for the sake of any earthly
honor and power, unless by force and compulsion. Upon
this he said: 'If you cannot accede to this, at least grant
me half your service: spend six months with me here, and
six in Wales.' To this I replied: 'I could not easily or
rashly promise even that without the approval of my
friends.' At length, however, when I perceived that he
was really anxious for my services, though I knew not
why, I promised him that, if my life were spared, I would
return to him after six months, with such a reply as should
be agreeable to him as well as advantageous to me and
mine. With this answer he was satisfied; and when I had
given him a pledge to return at the appointed time, on the
fourth day we rode away from him, and returned to my
own country. After our departure, a violent fever seized
me in the city of Cærwent,[1] where I lay for twelve months
and one week, night and day, without hope of recovery.
When at the appointed time, therefore, I had not fulfilled
my promise of visiting him, he sent letters to hasten my
journey on horseback to him, and to inquire the cause of
my delay. As I was unable to ride to him, I sent a reply
to make known to him the cause of my delay, and assure
him that, if I recovered from my illness, I would fulfil what
I had promised. My disease finally left me, and accordingly, by the advice and consent of all my friends, for the
benefit of that holy place and of all who dwelt therein,
I devoted myself to the king's service as I had promised, the
condition being that I should remain with him six months

---

[1] Five miles southwest of Chepstow. 'There was an abbey there,
where a traveling ecclesiastic would be likely to stay, and it was on
the great Roman road to South Wales, by which a traveler from Wessex to St. Davids would proceed' (Stevenson).

every year, either continuously, if I could spend six months with him at once, or alternately, three months in Wales and three in Wessex. It was also understood that he should in all ways be helpful to St. Davids, as far as his power extended.[1] For my friends hoped by this means to sustain less tribulation and harm from King Hemeid — who often plundered that monastery and the parish of St. Davids, and sometimes expelled the bishops who ruled over it, as he did Archbishop Nobis, my relative, and on occasion myself, their subordinate — if in any way I could secure the notice and friendship of the king.

80. The Welsh Princes who submit to Alfred.[2] — At that time, and long before, all the countries in South Wales belonged to King Alfred, and still belong to him. For instance, King Hemeid, with all the inhabitants of the region of Dyfed,[3] restrained by the violence of the six sons of Rhodri,[4] had submitted to the dominion of the king. Howel also, son of Ris, King of Glywyssing,[5] and Brochmail and Fernmail, sons of Mouric, kings of Gwent,[6] compelled by the violence and tyranny of Ealdorman Æthelred and of the Mercians, of their own accord sought out the same king,[7] that they might enjoy rule and protection from him against their enemies. Helised, also, son of Teudubr, King of Brecknock, compelled by the violence of the same sons of Rhodri, of his own accord sought the lordship of the

---

[1] The MS. seems to be corrupt at this point, so that what I have given is a loose conjectural rendering of the Latin: . . . *et illa adjuvaretur per rudimenta Sancti Dequi in omni causa, tamen pro viribus*.

[2] Original.

[3] Pembrokeshire and part of Carmarthenshire.

[4] 'Rhodri Mawr (the Great), King of Gwyneth, who acquired the rule of the whole of North and Mid-Wales and Cardigan' (Stevenson).

[5] Old name of Glamorgan and part of Monmouthshire.

[6] In Monmouthshire.   [7] Alfred.

aforesaid king; and Anarawd, son of Rhodri, with his brothers, at length abandoning the friendship of the Northumbrians, from whom he had received no good, but rather harm, came into King Alfred's presence, and eagerly sought his friendship. The king received him with honor, adopted him as his son by confirmation from the bishop's hand,[1] and bestowed many gifts upon him. Thus he became subject to the king with all his people, on condition that he should be obedient to the king's will in all respects, in the same way as Æthelred and the Mercians.

81. How Alfred rewards Submission.[2] — Nor was it in vain that they all gained the friendship of the king. For those who desired to augment their worldly power obtained power; those who desired money gained money; those who desired his friendship acquired his friendship; those who wished more than one secured more than one. But all of them had his love and guardianship and defense from every quarter, so far as the king, with all his men, could defend himself. When therefore I had come to him at the royal vill called Leonaford,[3] I was honorably received by him, and remained that time with him at his court eight months; during which I read to him whatever books he liked, of such as he had at hand; for this is his peculiar and most confirmed habit, both night and day, amid all his other occupations of mind and body,[4] either himself to read books, or to listen to the reading of others. And when I frequently had sought his permission to return, and had in no

---

[1] See chaps. 8 and 56.   [2] Original.

[3] Perhaps Landford in Wiltshire.

[4] In Alfred's Preface to his translation of Boethius we are told: '[He made this translation as well as he could], considering the various and manifold worldly cares that oft troubled him both in mind and body.' The similarity of phrase is striking.

way been able to obtain it, at length, when I had made up
my mind by all means to demand it, he called me to him at
twilight on Christmas Eve, and gave me two letters in which
was a manifold list of all the things which were in the two
monasteries which are called in Saxon Congresbury and
Banwell[1]; and on that same day he delivered to me those
two monasteries with everything in them, together with a
silken pallium of great value, and of incense a load for a
strong man, adding these words, that he did not give me
these trifling presents because he was unwilling hereafter
to give me greater. For in the course of time he unexpect-
edly gave me Exeter, with the whole diocese which belonged
to him in Wessex and in Cornwall, besides gifts every day
without number of every kind of worldly wealth; these it
would be too long to enumerate here, lest it should weary
my readers. But let no one suppose that I have mentioned
these presents in this place for the sake of glory or flattery,
or to obtain greater honor; I call God to witness that I
have not done so, but that I might certify to those who are
ignorant how profuse he was in giving. He then at once
gave me permission to ride to those two monasteries, so full
of all good things, and afterwards to return to my own.

82. The Siege of Paris.[2] — In the year of our Lord's incarnation 886, which was the thirty-eighth of King Alfred's
life, the army so often mentioned again fled the country,
and went into that of the West Franks. Entering the
river Seine with their vessels, they sailed up it as far as the
city of Paris; there they wintered, pitching their camp on
both sides of the river almost to the bridge, in order that
they might prevent the citizens from crossing the bridge —
since the city occupies a small island in the middle of the

---

[1] Both in Somersetshire; these monasteries are otherwise unknown.
[2] Largely from the *Chronicle*.

stream. They besieged the city for a whole year, but, by the merciful favor of God, and by reason of the brave defense of the citizens, they could not force their way inside the walls.

83. Alfred rebuilds London.[1] — In that same year Alfred, King of the Anglo-Saxons, after the burning of cities and massacres of the people, honorably rebuilt the city of London, made it habitable, and gave it into the custody of Æthelred, Ealdorman of Mercia. To this king[2] all the Angles and Saxons who hitherto had been dispersed everywhere, or were in captivity with the heathen,[3] voluntarily turned, and submitted themselves to his rule.[4]

84. The Danes leave Paris.[5] — In the year of our Lord's incarnation 887, which was the thirty-ninth of King Alfred's life, the above-mentioned army of the heathen, leaving the city of Paris uninjured, since otherwise they could get no advantage, passed under the bridge and rowed their fleet up the river Seine for a long distance, until they reached the mouth of the river Marne; here they left the Seine, entered the mouth of the Marne, and, sailing up it for a good distance and a good while, at length, not without labor, arrived at a place called Chézy, a royal vill, where they wintered a whole year. In the following year they entered the mouth of the river Yonne, not without doing much damage to the country, and there remained one year.

85. Division of the Empire.[6] — In that same year Charles,[7] King of the Franks, went the way of all flesh; but Arnolf,

---

[1] Largely from the *Chronicle*.   [2] Namely, Alfred.
[3] A mistranslation from the *Chronicle*; it should read, 'were not in captivity,' etc.
[4] Here follows Camden's famous (forged?) interpolation about Grimbald and Oxford.   [6] From the *Chronicle*,
[5] Much expanded from the *Chronicle*.   [7] Charles the Fat.

his brother's son, six weeks before he died, had expelled him from the kingdom. Immediately after his death five kings were ordained, and the kingdom was split into five parts; but the principal seat of the kingdom justly and deservedly fell to Arnolf, were it not that he had shamefully sinned against his uncle. The other four kings promised fidelity and obedience to Arnolf, as was meet; for none of these four kings was heir to the kingdom on his father's side, as was Arnolf; therefore, though the five kings were ordained immediately upon the death of Charles, yet the Empire remained to Arnolf. Such, then, was the division of that realm; Arnolf received the countries to the east of the river Rhine; Rudolf the inner part of the kingdom[1]; Odo the western part; Berengar and Wido, Lombardy, and those countries which are on that side of the mountain. But they did not keep such and so great dominions in peace among themselves, for they twice fought a pitched battle, and often mutually ravaged those kingdoms, and drove one another out of their dominions.

86. Alfred sends Alms to Rome.[2] — In the same year in which that army left Paris and went to Chézy,[3] Æthelhelm, Ealdorman of Wiltshire, carried to Rome the alms of King Alfred and of the Saxons.

87. Alfred begins to translate from Latin.[4] — In that same year also the oft-mentioned Alfred, King of the Anglo-Saxons, by divine inspiration first began, on one and the same day, to read and to translate; but that this may be clearer to those who are ignorant, I will relate the cause of this long delay in beginning.

88. Alfred's Manual.[5] — On a certain day we were both of us sitting in the king's chamber, talking on all kinds of

---

[1] Burgundy.   [2] Chiefly from the *Chronicle*.
[3] Cf. chap. 84.   [4] Original.   [5] Original.

subjects, as usual, and it happened that I read to him a quotation out of a certain book. While he was listening to it attentively with both ears, and pondering it deeply with his inmost mind, he suddenly showed me a little book[1] which he carried in his bosom, wherein were written the daily course, together with certain Psalms and prayers which he had read in his youth, and thereupon bade me write the quotation in that book. Hearing this, and perceiving in part his active intelligence and goodness of heart, together with his devout resolution of studying divine wisdom, I gave, though in secret, yet with hands uplifted to heaven, boundless thanks to Almighty God, who had implanted such devotion to the study of wisdom in the king's heart. But since I could find no blank space in that book wherein to write the quotation, it being all full of various matters, I delayed a little, chiefly that I might stir up the choice understanding of the king to a higher knowledge of the divine testimonies. Upon his urging me to make haste and write it quickly, I said to him, 'Are you willing that I should write that quotation on some separate leaf? Perhaps we shall find one or more other such which will please you; and if that should happen, we shall be glad that we have kept this by itself.' 'Your plan is good,' said he; so I gladly made haste to get ready a pamphlet of four leaves, at the head of which I wrote what he had bidden me; and that same day I wrote in it, at his request, and as I had predicted, no less than three other quotations which pleased him. From that time we daily talked together, and investigated the same subject by the help of other quotations which we found and which pleased him, so that the pamphlet gradually became full, and deservedly so, for it is written, 'The righteous man builds upon a

[1] Cf. chap. 24.

moderate foundation, and by degrees passes to greater things.'[1] Thus, like a most productive bee, flying far and wide, and scrutinizing the fenlands, he eagerly and unceasingly collected various flowers of Holy Scripture, with which he copiously stored the cells of his mind.[2]

89. Alfred's Handbook.[3] — When that first quotation had been copied, he was eager at once to read, and to translate into Saxon, and then to teach many others — even as we are assured concerning that happy thief who recognized the Lord Jesus Christ, his Lord, aye, the Lord of all men, as he was hanging on the venerable gallows of the holy cross, and, with trustful petition, casting down of his body no more than his eyes, since he was so entirely fastened with nails that he could do nothing else, cried with humble voice, 'O Christ, remember me when thou comest into thy kingdom!'[4] — since it was only on the cross that he began to learn the elements of the Christian faith.[5] Inspired by God, he began the rudiments of Holy Scripture on the sacred feast of St. Martin.[6] Then he went on, as far as he was able, to learn the flowers[7] collected from various quarters by any and all of his teachers, and to reduce them into the form of one book, although jumbled together, until it became almost as large as a psalter. This book he called his Enchiridion[8]

---

[1] Author unknown.   [3] Original.
[2] Cf. chap. 76.   [4] Luke 23. 42.
[5] The following phrases, introduced at this point, seem to be corrupt: *Hic aut aliter, quamvis dissimili modo, in regia potestate.*
[6] November 11.
[7] Alfred calls the passages which he translated from St. Augustine's *Soliloquies* by the name of 'flowers' or 'blossoms' (*blōstman*). See Hargrove's edition (*Yale Studies in English* XIII), and his version into modern English (*Yale Studies in English* XXII).
[8] The application of the word to a work of St. Augustine's gave it great currency in the Frankish Latin of the period.

or Handbook,[1] because he carefully kept it at hand day and night, and found, as he then used to say, no small consolation therein.

90. Illustration from the Penitent Thief.[2] — But, as it was written by a wise man,[3]

> Of watchful minds are they whose pious care
> It is to govern well,

I see that I must be especially watchful, in that I just now drew a kind of comparison, though in dissimilar manner,[4] between the happy thief and the king; for the cross is hateful to every one in distress.[5] But what can he do, if he cannot dislodge himself or escape thence ? or in what way can he improve his condition by remaining there? He must, therefore, whether he will or no, endure with pain and sorrow that which he is suffering.

91. Alfred's Troubles.[6] — Now the king was pierced with many nails of tribulation, though established in the royal sway; for from the twentieth year of his age to the present year, which is his forty-fifth,[7] he has been constantly afflicted with most severe attacks of an unknown disease, so that there is not a single hour in which he is not either suffering from that malady, or nigh to despair by reason of the gloom which is occasioned by his fear of it. Moreover the constant invasions of foreign nations, by which he was continually harassed by land and sea, without any interval of quiet, constituted a sufficient cause of disturbance.

What shall I say of his repeated expeditions against the heathen, his wars, and the incessant occupations of

---

[1] The Handbook seems to have been known to William of Malmesbury (d. 1143); cf. his *Gesta Pontificum*, pp. 333, 336.
[2] Original. [3] Unknown. [4] Cf. note 5, chap. 89.
[5] . . . *unicuique ubicumque male habet.* [6] Original. [7] Cf . chap. 74.

government ? Of the daily . . . of the[1] nations which dwell
on[2] the Tyrrhene[3] Sea to the farthest end of Ireland ? For
we have seen and read letters, accompanied with presents,
which were sent to him from Jerusalem by the patriarch
Elias.[4] What shall I say of his restoration of cities and
towns, and of others which he built where none had been
before? of golden and silver buildings,[5] built in incompa-
rable style under his direction? of the royal halls and
chambers, wonderfully erected of stone and wood at his
command? of the royal vills constructed of stones removed
from their old site, and finely rebuilt by the king's command in more fitting places?

Not to speak of the disease above mentioned, he was
disturbed by the quarrels of his subjects,[6] who would of
their own choice endure little or no toil for the common
need of the kingdom. He alone, sustained by the divine

[1] MS. corrupt: *De cotidiana nationum.*

[2] This makes no sense; yet the Latin is: *quæ in Tyrreno mari usque
ultimum Hibernæ finem habitant.*

[3] Cf. chap. 70.

[4] Perhaps Elias III, patriarch from about 879 to 907; the MS. reads
Abel. Stevenson's emendation is supported by the fact that certain
medical recipes are related to have been sent to Alfred by the patriarch
Elias (Cockayne, *Leechdoms* 2. 290).

[5] Stevenson says: 'Possibly he intended to refer to the use of the precious metals in sacred edifices. We are told, on the doubtful authority
of William of Malmesbury, that King Ine built a chapel of gold and
silver at Glastonbury. A ninth-century writer records that Ansegis,
abbot of Fontenelle, 806-833, partly decorated a spire of the abbey with
gilt metal, and another writer of that period mentions the golden doors
of the "basilica" of St. Alban in his description of the imperial palace
at Ingelheim. Giraldus Cambrensis ascribes the use of golden roofs or
roof-crests to the Romans at Caerleon-on-Usk. The idea that a king's
palace ought to be decorated with the precious metals is probably an
outcome of the late Roman rhetoric and Byzantine magnificence.'

[6] The early part of the sentence is corrupt in the MS.

aid, once he had assumed the helm of government, strove
in every way, like a skilful pilot, to steer[1] his ship, laden
with much wealth, into the safe and longed-for harbor of
his country, though almost all his crew were weary, suffering them not to faint or hesitate, even amid the waves
and manifold whirlpools of this present life. Thus his
bishops, earls, nobles, favorite thanes, and prefects, who,
next to God and the king, had the whole government of
the kingdom, as was fitting, continually received from him
instruction, compliment, exhortation, and command; nay,
at last, if they were disobedient, and his long patience was
exhausted, he would reprove them severely, and censure
in every way their vulgar folly and obstinacy; and thus
he wisely gained and bound them to his own wishes and
the common interests of the whole kingdom. But if, owing
to the sluggishness of the people, these admonitions of the
king were either not fulfilled, or were begun late at the
moment of necessity, and so, because they were not carried
through, did not redound to the advantage of those who
put them in execution — take as an example the fortresses
which he ordered, but which are not yet begun or, begun
late, have not yet been completely finished — when hostile
forces have made invasions by sea, or land, or both, then
those who had set themselves against the imperial orders
have been put to shame and overwhelmed with vain repentance. I speak of vain repentance on the authority of
Scripture, whereby numberless persons have had cause for
sorrow when they have been smitten by great harm through
the perpetration of deceit. But though by this means, sad
to say, they may be bitterly afflicted, and roused to grief by
the loss of fathers, wives, children, thanes, man servants,
maid servants, products, and all their household stuff,

---

[1] The figure is found as early as Sophocles and Aristophanes.

what is the use of hateful repentance when their kinsmen are dead, and they cannot aid them, or redeem from dire captivity those who are captive? for they cannot even help themselves when they have escaped, since they have not wherewithal to sustain their own lives. Sorely exhausted by a tardy repentance, they grieve over their carelessness in despising the king's commands; they unite in praising his wisdom, promising to fulfil with all their might what before they had declined to do, namely, in the construction of fortresses, and other things useful to the whole kingdom.

92. Alfred builds two Monasteries.[1] — Concerning his desire and intent of excellent meditation, which, in the midst both of prosperity and adversity, he never in any way neglected, I cannot in this place with advantage forbear to speak. For, when he was reflecting, according to his wont, upon the need of his soul,[2] he ordered, among the other good deeds to which his thoughts were by night and day[3] especially turned, that two monasteries should be built, one of them being for monks at Athelney.[4] This is a place surrounded by impassable fens and waters on every hand, where no one can enter but by boats, or by a bridge laboriously constructed between two fortresses, at the western end of which bridge was erected a strong citadel, of beautiful work, by command of the aforesaid king. In this monastery he collected monks of all kinds from every quarter, and there settled them.

---

[1] Original.

[2] This corresponds to the OE. *sāwle þearf*.

[3] The Latin has: *inter cetera diuturna et noctuma bona*. Stevenson does not emend, but it seems as though we should read *diurna*. Compare, for example, in Stevenson's edition, **78**. 14, 35, 39; **99**. 10; **100**. 11; **103**. 9.

[4] Cf . chap. 55. The second monastery was for nuns, and at Shaftesbury; see chap. 98.

93. Monasticism was decayed.[1] — At first he had no one of
his own nation, noble and free by birth, who was willing
to enter the monastic life, except children, who as yet could
neither choose good nor reject evil by reason of their tender
years. This was the case because for many years previous
the love of a monastic life had utterly decayed in that as
well as in many other nations; for, though many monasteries still remain in that country, yet no one kept the rule
of that kind of life in an orderly way, whether because of
the invasions of foreigners, which took place so frequently
both by sea and land, or because that people abounded in
riches of every kind, and so looked with contempt on the
monastic life. On this account it was that King Alfred
sought to gather monks of different kinds in the same
monastery.

94. Monks brought from beyond Sea.[2] — First he placed
there John[3] the priest and monk, an Old Saxon by birth,
making him abbot; and then certain priests and deacons
from beyond sea. Finding that he had not so large a number of these as he wished, he procured as many as possible
of the same Gallic race[4]; some of whom, being children,
he ordered to be taught in the same monastery, and at a
later period to be admitted to the monastic habit. I have
myself seen there in monastic dress a young man of heathen
birth who was educated in that monastery, and by no
means the hindmost of them all.

95. A Crime committed at Athelney.[5] — There was a crime
committed once in that monastery, which I would <not>,[6]
by my silence, utterly consign to oblivion, although it is
an atrocious villainy, for throughout the whole of Scripture

---

[1] Original.
[2] Original.
[3] Cf. chap. 78.
[4] Cf. chap. 78.
[5] Original.
[6] Supplied by Stevenson.

the base deeds of the wicked are interspersed among the reverend actions of the righteous, like tares and cockle among the wheat. Good deeds are recorded that they may be praised, imitated, and emulated, and that those who pursue them may be held worthy of all honor; and wicked deeds, that they may be censured, execrated, and avoided, and their imitators be reproved with all odium, contempt, and vengeance.

96. The Plot of a Priest and a Deacon.[1] — Once upon a time, a certain priest and a deacon, Gauls by birth, of the number of the aforesaid monks, by the instigation of the devil, and roused by jealousy, became so embittered in secret against their abbot, the above-mentioned John, that, after the manner of the Jews, they circumvented and betrayed their master. For they so wrought upon two hired servants of the same Gallic race that in the night, when all men were enjoying the sweet tranquillity of sleep, they should make their way into the church armed, and, shutting it behind them as usual, hide themselves there, and wait till the abbot should enter the church alone. At length, when, as was his wont, he should secretly enter the church by himself to pray, and, bending his knees, bow before the holy altar, the men should fall upon him, and slay him on the spot. They should then drag his lifeless body out of the church, and throw it down before the house of a certain harlot, as if he had been slain whilst on a visit to her. This was their device, adding crime to crime, as it is said, 'The last error shall be worse than the first.'[2] But the divine mercy, which is always wont to aid the innocent, frustrated in great part the evil design of those evil men, so that it did not turn out in all respects as they had planned.

[1] Original.   [2] Matt. 27. 64.

97. The Execution of the Plot.[1] — When, therefore, the whole of the evil teaching had been explained by those wicked teachers to their wicked hearers, and enforced upon them, the night having come and being favorable, the two armed ruffians, furnished with a promise of impunity, shut themselves up in the church to await the arrival of the abbot. In the middle of the night John, as usual, entered the church to pray, without any one's knowledge, and knelt before the altar. Thereupon the two ruffians rushed upon him suddenly with drawn swords, and wounded him severely. But he, being ever a man of keen mind, and, as I have heard say, not unacquainted with the art of fighting, if he had not been proficient in better lore, no sooner heard the noise of the robbers, even before he saw them, than he rose up against them before he was wounded, and, shouting at the top of his voice, struggled against them with all his might, crying out that they were devils and not men — and indeed he knew no better, as he thought that no men would dare to attempt such a deed. He was, however, wounded before any of his monks could come up. They, roused by the noise, were frightened when they heard the word 'devils'; being likewise unfamiliar with such struggles, they, and the two who, after the manner of the Jews, were traitors to their lord, rushed toward the doors of the church; but before they got there those ruffians escaped with all speed, and secreted themselves in the fens near by, leaving the abbot half dead. The monks raised their nearly lifeless superior, and bore him home with grief and lamentations; nor did those two knaves shed tears less than the innocent. But God's mercy did not allow so horrible a crime to pass unpunished: the desperadoes who perpetrated it, and all who urged them to it, were seized and bound; then, by

[1] Original.

various tortures, they died a shameful death. Let us now
return to our main narrative.

98. The Convent at Shaftesbury.[1] — Another[2] monastery
also was built by the aforesaid king as a residence for
nuns, near the eastern gate of Shaftesbury; and over it he
placed as abbess his own daughter Æthelgivu, a virgin
dedicated to God. With her many other noble ladies, serving God in the monastic life, dwell in that convent. These
two edifices were enriched by the king with much land,
and with all sorts of wealth.

99. Alfred divides his Time and his Revenues.[3] — These
things being thus disposed of, the king considered within
himself, as was his practice, what more would conduce to
religious meditation. What he had wisely begun and use-
fully conceived was adhered to with even more beneficial
result; for he had long before heard out of the book of the
law that the Lord[4] had promised to restore to him the
tenth many times over; and he knew that the Lord had
faithfully kept His promise, and had actually restored to
him the tithe manyfold. Encouraged by this precedent,
and wishing to surpass the practice of his predecessors, he
vowed humbly and faithfully to devote to God half his
services, by day and by night, and also half of all the
wealth which lawfully and justly came every year into his
possession; and this vow, as far as human discretion can
perceive and keep, he skilfully and wisely endeavored to
fulfil. But that he might, with his usual caution, avoid
that which Scripture warns us against, 'If thou offerest
aright, but dost not divide aright, thou sinnest,'[5] he considered how he might divide aright that which he had

---

[1] Original.   [3] Original.
[2] Cf. chap. 92.   [4] This passage is somewhat corrupt.
[5] Gen. 4. 7, in the old Latin version, following the Septuagint.

joyfully vowed to God; and as Solomon had said, 'The
king's heart is in the hand of the Lord'[1] — that is, his
counsel — he ordered with a divinely inspired policy, which
could come only from above, that his officers should first
divide into two parts the revenues of every year.

100. The Threefold Division of Officers at Court.[2] — After
this division had been made, he assigned the first part to
worldly uses, and ordered that one third of it should be
paid to his soldiers and to his officers, the nobles who dwelt
by turns at court, where they discharged various duties, for
thus it was that the king's household was arranged at all
times in three shifts,[3] in the following manner. The king's
attendants being wisely distributed into three companies,
the first company was on duty at court for one month,
night and day, at the end of which they were relieved by
the second company, and returned to their homes for two
months, where they attended to their own affairs. At the
end of the second month, the third company relieved the
second, who returned to their homes, where they spent
two months. The third company then gave place to the
first, and in their turn spent two months at home. And in
this order the rotation of service at the king's court was
at all times carried on.

101. The Distribution for Secular Purposes.[4] — To these,
therefore, was paid the first of the three portions aforesaid,
to each according to his standing and peculiar service; the
second to the workmen whom he had collected from many
nations and had about him in large numbers, men skilled
in every kind of building; the third portion was assigned

[1] Prov. 21. 1.   [2] Original.
[3] Cf. the *Chronicle* under 894: 'The King had divided his forces
into two, so that one half was constantly at home, the other half in the
field.'   [4] Original.

to foreigners who came to him out of every nation far and near; whether they asked money of him or not, he cheerfully gave to each with wonderful munificence according to their respective worthiness,[1] exemplifying what is written, 'God loveth a cheerful giver.'[2]

102. The Distribution for Religious Purposes.[3] — But the second part of all his revenues, which came yearly into his possession, and was included in the receipts of the exchequer, as I mentioned just above, he with full devotion dedicated to God, ordering his officers to divide it carefully into four equal parts with the provision that the first part should be discreetly bestowed on the poor of every nation who came to him; on this subject he said that, as far as human discretion could guarantee, the remark of Pope Gregory on the proper division of alms should be followed, 'Give not little to whom you should give much, nor much to whom little, nor nothing to whom something, nor something to whom nothing.'[4] The second share to the two monasteries which he had built, and to those who were serving God in them, as I have described more at length above. The third to the school[5] which he had studiously formed from many of the nobility of his own nation, but also from boys of mean condition. The fourth to the neighboring monasteries in all Wessex and Mercia, and also during some years, in turn, to the churches and servants of God dwelling in Wales, Cornwall,[6] Gaul,[7] Brittany, Northumbria,

---

[1] Or, 'rank' (*dignitatem*), as in line 3 of the chapter.

[2] 2 Cor. 9. 7.   [3] Original.

[4] Incorrectly quoted from the *Pastoral Care* 3. 20: 'Ne quædam quibus nulla, ne nulla quibus quædam, ne multa quibus pauca, ne pauca præbeant quibus impendere multa debuerunt.'

[5] See chaps. 75 and 76.   [7] See chaps. 78 and 94.

[6] See chaps. 74 and 81.

and sometimes, too, in Ireland; according to his means, he either distributed to them beforehand, or agreed to contribute afterwards, if life and prosperity did not fail him.

103. Alfred's Dedication of Personal Service.[1] — When the king had arranged all these matters in due order, he remembered the text of holy Scripture which says, 'Whosoever will give alms, ought to begin from himself,'[2] and prudently began to reflect what he could offer to God from the service of his body and mind; for he proposed to offer to God no less out of this than he had done of external riches.[3] Accordingly, he promised, as far as his infirmity and his means would allow, to render to God the half of his services, bodily and mental, by night and by day,[4] voluntarily, and with all his might. Inasmuch, however, as he could not distinguish with accuracy the lengths of the night hours in any way, on account of the darkness, nor frequently those of the day, on account of the thick clouds and rains, he began to consider by what regular means, free from uncertainty, relying on the mercy of God, he might discharge the promised tenor of his vow undeviatingly until his death.

104. Alfred's Measure of Time.[5] — After long reflection on these things, he at length, by a useful and shrewd invention, commanded his clerks[6] to supply wax in sufficient quantity, and to weigh it in a balance against pennies. When enough wax was measured out to equal the weight of seventy-two

---

[1] Original.

[2] Not from the Bible, but from St. Augustine's *Enchiridion de Fide*, chap. 20: 'Qui enim vult ordinate dare eleemosynam, a se ipso debet incipere.'

[3] Reading *divitiis* for the *divinis* of the text.

[4] Cf. chap. 99.   [5] Original.   [6] Or, 'chaplains.' See p. 41, note 5.

pence, he caused the clerks to make six candles thereof, all
of equal weight, and to mark off twelve inches as the
length of each candle.[1] By this plan, therefore, those six
caudles burned for twenty-four hours, a night and a day,
without fail, before the sacred relics of many of God's
elect, which always accompanied him wherever he went.
Sometimes, however, the candles could not continue burning a whole day and night, till the same hour when they
were lighted the preceding evening, by reason of the violence of the winds, which at times blew day and night
without intermission through the doors and windows[2] of
the churches, the sheathing, and the wainscot,[3] the numer-
ous chinks in the walls, or the thin material of the tents;
on such occasions it was unavoidable that they should burn
out and finish their course before the appointed hour. The
king, therefore, set himself to consider by what means he
might shut out the wind, and by a skilful and cunning
invention ordered a lantern to be beautifully constructed
of wood and ox-horn, since white ox-horns, when shaved
thin, are as transparent as a vessel of glass. Into this

---

[1] 'As these six candles weighed 72 pennyweights, each one was of
the weight of 12d. The weight of the OE. penny was 22 1/2 Troy grains,
so that each candle would weigh roughly 5/8 oz. avoirdupois. As the
candles were twelve inches long, they would be very thin in proportion
to their length. A modern beeswax candle burns at a considerably
quicker rate than is here assumed, but we do not think this condemns
the figures given in this chapter as imaginary. The candle of Alfred's
time was probably not moulded, and the wick would not be made of
cotton, as in the modern ones. Rushes, tow, and the hards of flax were
used for wicks. Aldhelm refers to the use of linen or flax wicks, but
also to those made of rushes. It is therefore hardly possible to repro-
duce the candles used by Alfred for the purpose of testing this chapter' (Stevenson).

[2] Reading *fenestras* for the *fenestrarum* of the text.

[3] Meanings doubtful.

lantern, then, wonderfully made of wood and horn, as I before said, a candle was put at night, which shone as brightly without as within, and was not disturbed by the wind, since he had also ordered a door of horn to be made for the opening of the lantern.[1] By this contrivance, then, six candles, lighted in succession, lasted twenty-four hours, neither more nor less. When these were burned out, others were lighted.

105. Alfred judges the Poor with Equity.[2] — When all these things were properly arranged, the king, eager to hold to the half of his daily service, as he had vowed to God, and more also, if his ability on the one hand, and his malady on the other, would allow him, showed himself a minute investigator of the truth in all his judgments, and this especially for the sake of the poor, to whose interest, day and night, among other duties of this life, he was ever wonderfully attentive. For in the whole kingdom the poor, besides him, had few or no helpers; for almost all the powerful and noble of that country had turned their thoughts rather to secular than to divine things: each was more bent on worldly business, to his own profit, than on the common weal.

106. His Correction of Unjust and Incompetent Judges.[2] — He strove also, in his judgments, for the benefit of both

---

[1] 'Ducange objected that horn lanterns were known to the Greeks and Romans long before Alfred's time. But the passages adduced by Salmasius, to whom he refers, and such others as we have been able to gather, do not clearly describe a horn lantern lit by a candle, but rather screens formed of horn to place round oil lamps. It is possible, therefore, that Alfred may really be the inventor of the horn lantern as we know it. The door in the side, which would be rendered necessary by the change of the candles every four hours, is here described, and seems to be a new feature' (Stevenson).

[2] Original.

his nobles and commons, who often quarreled fiercely among themselves at the meetings of the ealdormen and sheriffs, so that hardly one of them admitted the justice of what had been decided by these ealdormen and sheriffs. In consequence of this pertinacious and obstinate dissension, all felt constrained to give sureties to abide by the decision of the king, and both parties hastened to carry out their engagements. But if any one was conscious of injustice on his side in the suit, though by law and agreement he was compelled, however reluctant, to come for judgment before a judge like this, yet with his own good will he never would consent to come. For he knew that in that place no part of his evil practice would remain hidden; and no wonder, for the king was a most acute investigator in executing his judgments, as he was in all other things. He inquired into almost all the judgments which were given in his absence, throughout all his dominion, whether they were just or unjust. If he perceived there was iniquity in those judgments, he would, of his own accord, mildly ask those judges, either in his own person, or through others who were in trust with him, why they had judged so unjustly, whether through ignorance or malevolence — that is, whether for the love or fear of any one, the hatred of another, or the desire of some one's money. At length, if the judges acknowledged they had given such judgment because they knew no better, he discreetly and moderately reproved their inexperience and folly in such terms as these: 'I greatly wonder at your assurance, that whereas, by God's favor and mine, you have taken upon you the rank and office of the wise, you have neglected the studies and labors of the wise. Either, therefore, at once give up the administration of the earthly powers which you possess, or endeavor more zealously to study the lessons of wisdom.

Such are my commands.' At these words the ealdormen
and sheriffs would be filled with terror at being thus severely
corrected, and would endeavor to turn with all their might
to the study of justice, so that, wonderful to say, almost all
his ealdormen, sheriffs, and officers, though unlearned from
childhood, gave themselves up to the study of letters, choos-
ing rather to acquire laboriously an unfamiliar discipline
than to resign their functions. But if any one, from old age
or the sluggishness of an untrained mind, was unable to
make progress in literary studies, he would order his son,
if he had one, or one of his kinsmen, or, if he had no one
else, his own freedman or servant, whom he had long before
advanced to the office of reading, to read Saxon books
before him night and day, whenever he had any leisure.
And then they would lament with deep sighs from their
inmost souls that in their youth they had never attended to
such studies. They counted happy the youth of the present
day, who could be delightfully instructed in the liberal
arts, while they considered themselves wretched in that
they had neither learned these things in their youth, nor,
now they were old, were able to do so. This skill of young
and old in acquiring letters, I have set forth as a means of
characterizing the aforesaid king.

APPENDIXES

APPENDIX I

ALFRED'S PREFACE TO HIS TRANSLATION OF GREGORY'S PASTORAL CARE

THIS BOOK IS FOR WORCESTER[1]

King Alfred bids greet Bishop Wærferth with his words lovingly and with friendship; and I let it be known to thee that it has very often come into my mind what wise men there formerly were throughout England, both of sacred and secular orders; and what happy times there were then throughout England; and how the kings who had power over the nation in those days obeyed God and His ministers;how they preserved peace, morality, and order at home, and at the same time enlarged their territory abroad; and how they prospered both with war and with wisdom; and also how zealous the sacred orders were both in teaching and learning, and in all the services they owed to God; and how foreigners came to this land in search of wisdom and instruction, and how we should now have to get them from abroad if we were to have them. So general was its decay in England that there were very few on this side of the Humber who could understand their rituals in English, or translate a letter from Latin into English; and I believe that there were not many beyond the Humber. There were so few of them that I cannot remember a single one south of the Thames when I came to the throne. Thanks be to Almighty God that we have any teachers among us now. And therefore I command thee to do as I believe thou art willing, to disengage thyself from worldly matters as often as thou canst, that thou mayest apply the wisdom which God has given thee wherever thou canst. Consider what punishments would come upon us on account of this world, if we neither loved it [wisdom] ourselves nor suffered other men to obtain it: we should love

---

[1] The name of the diocese and of the bishop of course varied in the different copies.

the name only of Christian, and very few the virtues. When I
considered all this, I remembered also that I saw, before it had been
all ravaged and burned, how the churches throughout the whole of
England stood filled with treasures and books; and there was also a
great multitude of God's servants, but they had very little knowledge of the books, for they could not understand anything of them,
because they were not written in their own language. As if they
had said: 'Our forefathers, who formerly held these places, loved
wisdom, and through it they obtained wealth and bequeathed it to
us. In this we can still see their tracks, but we cannot follow
them, and therefore we have lost both the wealth and the wisdom,
because we would not incline our hearts after their example.'
When I remembered all this, I wondered extremely that the good
and wise men who were formerly all over England, and had per-
fectly learned all the books, had not wished to translate them into
their own language. But again I soon answered myself and said:
'They did not think that men would ever be so careless, and that
learning would so decay; through that desire they abstained from
it, since they wished that the wisdom in this land might increase
with our knowledge of languages.' Then I remembered how the
law was first known in Hebrew, and again, when the Greeks
had learned it, they translated the whole of it into their own language, and all other books besides. And again the Romans, when
they had learned them, translated the whole of them by learned
interpreters into their own language. And also all other Christian nations translated a part of them into their own language.
Therefore it seems better to me, if you think so, for us also
to translate some books which are most needful for all men to
know into the language which we can all understand, and for
you to do as we very easily can if we have tranquillity enough,
that is, that all the youth now in England of free men, who are
rich enough to be able to devote themselves to it, be set to
learn as long as they are not fit for any other occupation, until
they are able to read English writing well: and let those be
afterwards taught more in the Latin language who are to continue in learning, and be promoted to a higher rank. When I
remembered how the knowledge of Latin had formerly decayed
throughout England, and yet many could read English writing,
I began, among other various and manifold troubles of this

kingdom, to translate into English the book which is called in
Latin *Pastoralis,* and in English *Shepherd's Book,* sometimes word
by word, and sometimes according to the sense, as I had learned it
from Plegmund my archbishop, and Asser my bishop, and Grimbald my mass-priest, and John my mass-priest. And when I had
learned it as I could best understand it, and as I could most clearly
interpret it, I translated it into English; and I will send a copy
to every bishopric in my kingdom; and in each there is a book-
mark worth fifty mancuses.[1] And I command in God's name that
no man take the book-mark from the book, or the book from the
monastery. It is uncertain how long there may be such learned
bishops as now, thanks be to God, there are nearly everywhere;
therefore I wish them[2] always to remain in their places, unless the
bishop wish to take them with him, or they be lent out anywhere,
or any one be making a copy from them.

[1] Cf. p. 11, note 2.   [2] The books.

APPENDIX II

LETTER FROM FULCO, ARCHBISHOP OF RHEIMS AND PRIMATE OF THE FRANKS, AND *LEGATUS NATUS* OF THE APOSTOLIC SEE, TO ALFRED, THE MOST CHRISTIAN KING OF THE ANGLES[1]

To Alfred, the most glorious and most Christian King of the Angles, Fulco, by the grace of God Archbishop of Rheims, and servant of the servants of God, wisheth both the sceptre of temporal dominion, ever triumphant, and the eternal joys of the kingdom of heaven.

And first of all we give thanks to our Lord God, the Father of lights, and the Author of all good, from whom is every good gift and every perfect gift, who by the grace of His Holy Spirit hath not only been pleased to cause the light of His knowledge to shine in your heart, but also even now hath vouchsafed to kindle the fire of His love, by which at once enlightened and warmed, you earnestly tender the weal of the kingdom committed to you from above, by warlike achievements, with divine assistance attaining or securing peace for it, and desiring to extend the excellency of the ecclesiastical order, which is the army of God. Wherefore we implore the divine mercy with unwearied prayers that He who hath moved and warmed your heart to this

---

1 From Rev. Joseph Stevenson's translation of *The Book of Hyde*, in *Church Historians of England* (London, 1854), Vol. 2, Part 2, pp. 499-503. The translator states that the text of the letter printed by Wise in his edition of Asser (see Stevenson's edition of Asser, p. 308) 'has been employed in correcting the many obscurities and errors of the copy inserted in the *Liber de Hida*.' Of the letter our editor says: 'It . . . seems to be genuine. There is no conceivable motive for forging such a letter. We can discover no grounds for Pauli's condemnation of it. . . . As Malmesbury, *Gesta Regum*, c. 122 (p. 130), states that Grimbald was sent to Alfred at his request by the Archbishop of Rheims, he would seem to have been acquainted with this letter.'

would give effect to your wishes, by replenishing your desire with good things, that in your days both peace may be multiplied to your kingdom and people, and that ecclesiastical order, which as you say hath been disturbed in many ways, either by the continued irruptions and attacks of the pagans, or by lapse of years, or by the negligence of prelates, or by the ignorance of subjects, may by your diligence and industry be speedily reestablished, exalted, and diffused.

And since you wish this to be effected chiefly through our assistance, and since from our see, over which St. Remigius, the apostle of the Franks, presides, you ask for counsel and protection, we think that this is not done without divine impulse. And as formerly the nation of the Franks obtained by the same St. Remigius deliverance from manifold error, and the knowledge of the worship of the only true God, so doth the nation of the Angles request that it may obtain from his see and doctrine one by whom they may be taught to avoid superstition, to cut off superfluities, and to extirpate all such noxious things as bud forth from violated custom or rude habits, and may learn, while they walk through the field of the Lord, to pluck the flowers, and to be upon their guard against the adder.

For St. Augustine, the first bishop of your nation, sent to us by your apostle St. Gregory, could not in a short time set forth all the decrees of the holy apostles, nor did he think proper suddenly to burden a rude and barbarous nation with new and strange enactments; for he knew how to adapt himself to their infirmities, and to say with the Apostle, 'I have given milk to you to drink, who are babes in Christ, and not meat' (1 Cor. 3. 2). And as Peter and James, who were looked upon as pillars (Gal. 2. 9), with Barnabas and Paul, and the rest who were met together, did not wish to oppress the primitive Church, which was flowing in from the Gentiles to the faith of Christ, with a heavier burden than to command them to abstain from things offered to idols, and from fornication, and from things strangled, and from blood (Acts 15. 29), so also do we know how matters were managed with you at the beginning. For they required only this for training up the people in the knowledge of God, and turning them from their former barbarous fierceness, namely, that faithful and prudent servants should be placed over the Lord's household, who

should be competent to give out to each of their fellow-servants
his dole of food in due season, that is, according to the capacity
of each of the hearers. But in process of time, as the Christian
religion gained strength, the holy Church felt it neither to be her
inclination nor her duty to be satisfied with this, but to take
example from the apostles themselves, their masters and founders,
who, after the doctrines of the Gospel had been set forth and
spread abroad by their heavenly Master Himself, did not deem it
superfluous and needless, but convenient and salutary, to establish the perfect believers by frequent epistolary exhortations, and
to build them more firmly upon the solid foundation, and to
impart to them more abundantly the rule as well of manners as
of faith.

Nevertheless, she too, whether excited by adverse circum-
stances, or nourished by prosperous ones, never ceased to aim at
the good of her children, whom she is daily bringing forth to Christ,
and, inflamed by the fire of the Holy Spirit, to promote their
advancement, both privately and publicly. Hence the frequent
calling of councils, not only from the neighboring cities and
provinces, but also, in these days, from regions beyond seas; hence
synodal decrees so often published; hence sacred canons, framed
and consecrated by the Holy Spirit, by which both the Catholic
faith is powerfully strengthened, and the unity of the Church's
peace is inviolably guarded, and its order is decently regulated:
which canons, as it is unlawful for any Christian to transgress,
so it is altogether wicked, in clerk and priest especially, to be
ignorant of them; the wholesome observance and the religious
handing down of which are things ever to be embraced. Seeing
that, for the reasons above stated, all these matters have either
not been fully made known to your nation, or have now for the
most part failed, it hath appeared fit and proper to your Majesty
and to your royal wisdom, by a most excellent counsel — inspired,
as we believe, from above — both to consult us, insignificant as
we are, on this matter, and to repair to the see of St. Remigius,
by whose virtues and doctrine the same see or church hath always
flourished and excelled all the churches of Gaul since his time
in all piety and doctrine.

And since you are unwilling to appear before us, when you
present these your requests, without a gift and empty-handed,

your Majesty hath deigned to honor us with a present that is both
very necessary for the time and well suited to the matter in hand;
concerning which we have both praised heavenly Providence with
admiration, and have returned no slender thanks to your royal
munificence. For you have sent unto us a present of dogs, which,
of good and excellent breed, are yet only in the body and mortal;
and this you do that they may drive away the fury of visible
wolves, with which, among other scourges, wielded against us by
the righteous judgment of God, our country abounds; and you
ask us, in return, that we should send to you certain watch-
dogs, not corporeal, that is to say, not such as those with whom
the prophet finds fault, saying, 'Dumb dogs, not able to bark'
(Isa. 56. 10), but such as the Psalmist speaks of, 'That the
tongue of thy dogs may be red through the same' (Ps. 68. 23),
who know how and are qualified to make loud barkings for
their Lord, and constantly to guard His flock with most wakeful
and most careful watchings, and to drive away to a distance
those most cruel wolves of unclean spirits who lie in wait to
devour souls.

Of which number you specially demand one from us, namely,
Grimbald, priest and monk, to be sent for this office, and to pre-
side over the government of the pastoral charge. To whom the
whole Church, which hath nourished him, gives her testimony
from his childhood, with true faith and holy religion, and which
hath advanced him by regular steps, according to ecclesiastical
custom, to the dignity of the priesthood. We affirm openly that
he is most deserving of the honor of the episcopate, and that he
is fit to teach others also. But indeed we wished that this might
rather take place in our kingdom, and we intended some time
ago, with Christ's permission, to accomplish it in due time, namely,
that he whom we had as a faithful son we might have as an
associate in our office, and a most trustworthy assistant in everything that pertained to the advantage of the Church. It is not
without deep sorrow — forgive us for saying so — that we suffer him to be torn from us, and be removed from our eyes by so
vast an extent of land and sea. But as love has no perception
of loss, nor faith of injury, and no remoteness of regions can
part those whom the tie of unfeigned affection joins together,
we have most willingly assented to your request — for to you we

have no power to refuse anything — nor do we grudge him to you, whose advantage we rejoice in as much as if it were our own, and whose profit we count as ours: for we know that in every place one only God is served, and that the Catholic and Apostolic Church is one, whether it be at Rome or in the parts beyond the sea.

It is our duty, then, to make him over to you canonically; and it is your duty to receive him reverentially, that is to say, in such way and mode as may best conduce to the glory of your kingdom, to the honor of the Church and our prelacy; and to send him to you along with his electors, and with certain nobles and great personages of your kingdom, as well bishops, presbyters, deacons, as religious laymen also, who with their own lips promise and declare to us in the presence of our whole church that they will treat him with fitting respect during the whole course of his life, and that they will inviolably keep with the strictest care the canonical decrees and the rules of the Church, handed down to the Church by the apostles and by apostolic men, such as they could then hear from us, and afterwards learn from him their pastor and teacher, according to the form delivered by us to him. Which when they shall have done, with the divine blessing and the authority of St. Remigius, by our ministry and the laying on of hands, according to the custom of the Church, receiving him properly ordained, and in all things fully instructed, let them conduct him with due honor to his own seat, glad and cheerful themselves that they are always to enjoy his protection, and constantly to be instructed by his teaching and example.

And as the members feel a concern for each other, and when even one rejoices they rejoice with it, or if even one suffer all the other members sympathize with it, we again earnestly and specially commend him to your Royal Highness and to your most provident goodness, that he may be always permitted, with unfettered authority, without any gainsaying, to teach and to carry into effect whatever he may discover to be fit and useful for the honor of the Church and the instruction of your people, according to the authority of the canons and the custom of our Church, lest, haply — which God forbid! — any one, under the instigation of the devil, being moved by the impulse of spite and malevolence, should excite controversy or raise sedition against him. But should this happen, it will be your duty then to make special provision against this, and by all means to discourage by your royal censure all such persons, if they should chance to show themselves, and check barbaric rudeness by the curb of your authority; and it will be his duty always to consult for the salvation of the people committed to his pastoral skill, and rather to draw all men after him by love than to drive them by fear.

May you, most illustrious, most religious, and most invincible king, ever rejoice and flourish in Christ the Lord of lords.

INDEX

[The numbers refer to pages.]

Printed in Great Britain
by Amazon

36292060R00056